The Rolling Stones

The Rolling Stones

Tim Dowley

HIPPOCRENE BOOKS INC.
New York

Other popular music biographies

Bob Dylan: From a Hard Rain to a Slow Train Tim Dowley
and Barry Dunnage
Elvis Presley: A Study in Music Robert Matthew-Walker
Lennon & McCartney Malcolm Doney
The Nolans: In the Mood for Stardom Kim Treasurer
Frank Sinatra John Frayn Turner
Simon and Garfunkel Robert Matthew-Walker

The author and publisher are glad to acknowledge the
Keystone Press Agency, who supplied the photographs
included in this book.

First published in the UK in 1983 by
MIDAS BOOKS
12 Dene Way, Speldhurst
Tunbridge Wells, Kent TN3 0NX

ISBN 0 85936 234 5 (UK)

Published in USA by
HIPPOCRENE BOOKS INC
171 Madison Avenue
New York, NY 10016

ISBN 0-88254-734-8 (USA)

© Tim Dowley 1983

All rights reserved. No part of this publication may be
reproduced, stored in a retrieval system, or transmitted, in any
form or by any means, electronic, mechanical, photocopying
or otherwise, without the prior permission of Midas Books.

Printed in Great Britain by
Biddles Ltd, Guildford, Surrey

To Robin and Nicholas

Contents

1

War Babies

For twenty years now the Rolling Stones have held centre stage as the Bad Boys of the rock scene. The sexy macho nasties. Their Satanic Majesties. The dirty dreamers.

But to start we have to time-warp into another world: Dartford during the closing stages of the Second World War, where Michael Philip Jagger was born, on 26 July 1943.

Eva Jagger, his mother, was an Australian, but her family brought her to Britain while she was still a child. Her husband Joe Jagger, a Northerner, worked as a physical education teacher at a local secondary school. After Michael's birth Joe did military service, and Chris, their younger son, was not born till some years later.

Michael Jagger's primary school teacher, later a doting Stones fan, fills in some rose-tinted details about the years of austerity that followed the war. She claims that Michael's bright blue eyes, ginger hair and flirtatious smile were already captivating the women of Dartford. In contrast, his mother recollects a rebellious four-year-old who, on a family seaside holiday, demolished every sandcastle in sight.

As Joe Jagger's career prospered, the family moved up a rung on the social ladder to a house in Dartford West. Mick started school, attending Wentworth Primary, where Ella Smith was working as a temporary teacher. She claims that his spiky name – Mike (not Mick) Jagger – and spiky personality immediately stood out from the classroom clones confronting her. It was Mike, she boasts, who won her favour, with his impetuous enthusiasm. 'Miss, miss, I know, miss!'

Eva acquired the reputation of being a bit of a social climber. As an Australian, she resented the snubs she received from her English neighbours, and seemed determined to disprove their aspersions about her working-class roots. She strove to out-English the English middle-class suburbanites, and won another round in this contest when the Jaggers moved into a new detached house – complete with white pebbledash, french windows and its own little orchard – in the village of Wilmington, just outside Dartford. The trees gave young Mike and Chris a stage for their own Tarzan episodes, swinging through the branches with bloodcurdling cries, to the unvoiced terror of their mother. Mick himself reckons his mother is very working class, his father bourgeois, leaving him somewhere between the two. 'It's more of a hang-up making it if you're from the bourgeoisie.'

School was no real problem for Mike Jagger, and he successfully straddled the scholarship hurdles at the age of eleven, duly progressing to Dartford Grammar School. His brother Chris claims Mike detested compulsory games, the traditionally repulsive school dinners and the compulsory school uniform – but find an English grammar school boy who didn't. Chris also offers the priceless nugget that his older brother regularly got caught not wearing his school cap, and was given 'lines' as his punishment.

Although his father was a PE teacher, Mike could summon little enthusiasm for team games, especially the gratuitously violent rugby, though he did represent the school at basketball. His aversion for much of what grammar school stood for was reciprocated towards him by most of the masters; he was generally not liked, though his French and history teachers were apparently among the exceptions to this feeling. Despite this mutual distaste, Mike managed a creditable seven 'O' level GCEs.

Mike's mother did notice (or perhaps encourage) a streak of ambition in him from an early age. He apparently never admitted any deep yearning to become an engine driver or an aircraft pilot; his sights were set on making money. Mrs Jagger claims he was leader of his schoolmates, always ready to defend his beliefs, and she harboured secret visions of him as a budding politician or barrister. But such stuffy professions lacked appeal for Mike; they were no way to make money fast.

Mike Jagger's distaste for school was reflected in his full use of his spare time. When not chasing around 'trying to find girls who would screw', he was developing a taste for pop music. His brother Chris says he brought back a cheap guitar from a family holiday in Spain.

Apart from a restless energy, probably the only trait pointing to future developments was Mike's knack for mimicry. His family and friends noticed a perceptive ear and exceptional memory. Mrs Jagger reminisced: 'Ever since he was a little child of eleven or so he had this knack of listening to a hit song over the wireless just a few times and then he'd stand up and sing them over just like the originals . . . When he's imitating something, it has to be just right.' He used to listen to pop on the radio, from BBC to Radio Luxembourg, from Frankie Laine to Rosemary Clooney.

It was the discovery of rhythm and blues, when he was about fourteen, that began to spur Mike towards an increasing interest in music. He started by listening to records of pure blues singers – great names such as Big Bill Broonzy, Huddy 'Leadbelly' Ledbetter and Robert Johnson – from the American South. He passed on from them to the newer generation of urban rhythm and blues singers, and to their rock 'n' roll imitators, Chuck Berry, Little Richard and Bo Diddley. Such names were far from popular in Britain at this time; the stars were Pat Boone, Connie Francis and Ricky Nelson.

It was a shared fanaticism for rock that brought together Mike Jagger and another Dartford Grammar boy, Dick Taylor. They listened avidly to specially imported rock

11

albums: 'When I was thirteen the first person I really admired was Little Richard. I wasn't particularly fond of Elvis or Bill Hayley . . . I was more into Jerry Lee Lewis, Chuck Berry and a bit later Buddy Holly. There was a lot of TV then, *Cool for Cats*, *6.5 Special*, *Oh, Boy*, and I saw a lot of people on those shows.' (Jagger actually saw Buddy Holly on stage at the Woolwich Granada on a rare night out.) Dick and Mike also shared a taste for Leadbelly and Broonzy.

This music began to form a symbol of rebellion against Jagger's parents. His friends had sometimes been surprised at his knuckling under to his father; Joe Jagger, the physical education specialist, used to demand that his son complete a rigorous routine of physical jerks – press-ups, weightlifting, garden circuits and the rest – and Mike obeyed compliantly, even when Dick or other friends were impatiently waiting for him to join them for a music session. The idea of rejecting his father's demands had not been allowed to form in his mind. Yet when Joe Jagger suggested that Mike's musical tastes amounted to 'jungle music', Mike defiantly agreed. 'Yeah, that's right, jungle music. That's a very good description.'

It was with Dick Taylor that Mike formed the nucleus of what amounted to a skiffle group. Dick started out with an ancient drum kit inherited from his grandad. He then stepped up from this to a bass guitar. Unable to play an instrument, Jagger, eager to be a performer, settled for singing. As a vocalist he used his gift for mimicry to emulate the slurred tones of the American singers he favoured.

Jagger and Taylor were soon joined by others, and adopted the unlikely name 'Little Boy Blue and the Blue Boys'. They quickly achieved notoriety in quiet suburban Wilmington. At first Mrs Jagger found it all rather funny; she would 'crease up with laughter' at their efforts. But her sense of humour was quickly exhausted, and the group was ejected from the Jagger home. 'It's just that the neighbours are complaining . . . And I have to keep peace with the neighbours.'

Keith Richards was also born in Dartford, nearly six

months after Jagger, on 18 December 1943. (The 's' in the family name was dropped by Keith soon after the Rolling Stones began to make their mark as a band.) For a short time Keith and Mike lived close enough to become friends, but when the Richard family moved out of Dartford the two boys lost touch. It was at primary school that Keith first tasted stardom. His boy soprano voice was good enough to see him competing in school choir competitions at the Royal Albert Hall and singing in a cherubic white surplice at Westminster Abbey. He was among the best; only three boys were considered good enough to sing the 'hallelujahs'. 'That was my first taste of show business – when my voice broke, and they didn't want me in the choir any more. Suddenly it was, "Don't call us, we'll call you." I think that was when I stopped being a good boy and started to be a yob.'

Richard comes across as a loner and a rebel. In contrast with Jagger's ability as a school athlete, Keith played truant and avoided compulsory games. He hated rugby, and survived cross-country runs by dropping out near the start, finding a hidden spot for a quick smoke, and rejoining the exhausted and muddy runners as they came back towards the school.

Music seems to have put in an early appearance. We hear of a saxophone acquired at the age of seven, hauled around by its diminutive owner to the amusement of passers-by. When he was fifteen his mother bought him a £10 Spanish guitar, and this proved the turning point. His grandfather played country fiddle, and had a dance band before the war; he taught Keith the rudiments of the guitar, after which he made his own way.

If Jagger was disliked at grammar school, Richard was notorious at Dartford Technical School. He was eventually expelled for truancy, leaving him the alternatives of following his father into a job in electrical engineering or going to art college, the haven of many so-called misfits. Richard blames school for knocking the desire to learn out of him. In the event, he opted for the nearest art college, Sidcup Art School, where he met Dick Taylor, Jagger's friend from Dartford Grammar, who had similarly been attracted there by the promise of postponing having to find a job, and of not needing to work too hard.

Dick was still playing music with Jagger and the others, listening to records, and generally expanding his musical education. At Sidcup, where he was ostensibly training for a career in advertising, Keith found himself looked up to as a natural leader. His rebel stance – even before Sidcup he looked the part of a Teddy boy, with his drainpipe trousers, shocking pink socks and winkle-pickers – as well as his wild behaviour and fanatical enthusiasm for rhythm and blues, all singled him out.

Phil May, later singer with the Pretty Things, was another product of Sidcup Art School, and remembers Dick Taylor and Keith Richard practising on acoustic guitars in the lavatories during breaktime. The toilets rated high in Richard's evaluation of art school: 'I mean it's just great there, you go take a piss, and there's always some cat who's sneaked out to the bog and he's going through his latest Jack Elliott or Woody Guthrie number, and you discover Robert Johnson, and it all comes together for you. Art school is great – in the bog.'

Taylor regarded Richard as a hooligan, but none the worse for it. On an art school trip to study furniture design at the fashionable West End store of Heal's, Taylor watched in horrified fascination as Keith Richard deliberately dropped a burning cigarette on to an expensive display sofa. By now Richard had graduated from his Ted's outfit to a perennial lilac shirt, jeans and denim jacket.

It was a chance meeting at Dartford railway station in the spring of 1960 that really set things moving. By now, with seven 'O' levels and some good 'A' levels behind him, Mike Jagger had started a course at the London School of Economics in preparation for a career in accounting, and was commuting into town daily from his home in Kent. Keith happened to be travelling at the same time, carrying his guitar, and noticed the bundle of LPs that Jagger was clutching under his arm. They included a Chuck Berry album, *Back in the USA*, specially imported from Chess Studios in Chicago. That was enough to spark Keith's interest. The two soon got talking; but it was their shared musical tastes – Muddy Waters, Chuck Berry, Little Walter – rather than their boyhood memories that cemented their relationship. At this time, artists like these were still practically unknown to the majority.

Fired with enthusiasm, Keith asked Mike to bring some of his records round to his home, and told his friend Dick Taylor of his encounter, only to discover that Dick and Mike had been playing in the same group for months. After listening to some of the discs, they started playing music together. Jagger even invited Richard to join the Blue Boys, who were now beginning to find a characteristic sound of their own. Keith Richard's guitar playing was, not surprisingly, Chuck Berry-influenced, and Jagger was finding a vocal rawness suited to the blues. Bob Beckwith, an early member of the Blue Boys and another LSE student, pulled out, leaving Keith a place as second guitar. Allen Etherington was also a member of the Blue Boys at this stage.

It was the arrival of Keith Richard that brought up the notion of playing for money, not at first as a full-time professional group, but simply playing gigs to earn some useful extra cash. At first the others simply shrugged off the idea, but eventually burning enthusiasm for rhythm and blues, a hunger to perform, and Richard's drive combined to push them on.

It is important to remember the musical ethos of the period. In the late 1950s the BBC had scarcely admitted even the existence of pop, and the only 'alternative' radio was Luxembourg, with its top-ten obsession. Trad jazz and bland teeny-pop idols like Helen Shapiro and Adam Faith ruled unchallenged. Nobody was listening to rhythm and blues, gutsy black music.

Suddenly, early in 1962, there appeared in *Melody Maker* an announcement that Alexis Korner was about to open the Ealing Club, devoted to black music, in the back room of the ABC Bakery, Ealing. His own group, Blues Incorporated, the first English R&B band, was to be the regular group. This was enough. Jagger, Richard and Taylor, like many other scattered fans, found their way to Ealing to discover more.

Alexis Korner is a name to conjure with in British music. Chris Barber once said that his very *raison d'être* was to bring people together. Korner's influence has been extraordinary; groups as diverse as Pentangle, Led Zeppelin, Cream, Manfred Mann and McGuinness Flint have included former co-musicians of Korner's.

Blues Incorporated normally comprised Korner himself on guitar, Cyril Davies on harmonica, Charlie Watts on drums, Dick Heckstall-Smith on tenor sax, and Jack Bruce on bass. Korner, born in Paris of an Austrian father and Greco-Turkish mother, had been expelled from St Paul's School and thrown out of the Boy Scouts. Entering the music business, he played successively in Chris Barber's jazz band, Ken Colyer's skiffle group, and then in a duo with Cyril Davies, a North London panelbeater. They began experimenting with playing the blues in an R&B style on electric guitars, to the derision of most of their audiences.

Jagger and his crowd were impressed with what they heard at the Ealing Club, and particularly excited when a young blond guitarist joined in a jam session. It was soon clear that he was indebted to Elmore James' style of bar-slide guitar playing. Mike and Keith were so impressed that they lost no time in introducing themselves to the guitarist, Brian Jones, who was at this time calling himself 'Elmo Lewis'.

Jones had first contacted Korner when the latter was playing his home town, Cheltenham, with Chris Barber's band in 1961. At the time Jones had been playing in a local jazz band and working as an assistant in an architectural office. Brian soon took up Alexis' offer to put him up if he was in London; he came up to hear Blues Incorporated, and often slept on Korner's floor. In due course Brian moved to London, living in a succession of West London flats and working in department stores.

Brian Jones was probably the most enigmatic of the Rolling Stones. He was born in Cheltenham, most sedate of spa towns, on 28 February 1942, into a middle-class family. His father, a science graduate, was an aircraft engineer and played the organ at a local church; his mother was a piano teacher. By the age of ten his mother had passed on all she knew about piano playing to Brian, and lessons were arranged with a more advanced teacher. He took up the clarinet, and when he discovered Charlie Parker insisted on acquiring an alto sax, which he proceeded to teach himself to play. Brian was only disappointed that the sounds he made had so little in common with the amazing 'Bird'. Brian also owned a £3 Spanish guitar.

At first music was only one of a number of enthusiasms. Jones, like Jagger, was good at games – cricket, judo and diving – but got bored with them all too quickly. He was bright academically, and his parents looked forward to the possibility of university and a professional career. Instead of this he began to build up a strong emotional reaction against authority, which started to turn him away from conventional patterns of behaviour and to withdrawal into himself. One of his former schoolmasters commented, 'Brian was a boy who clearly got upset at any injustice. He worried when anybody else in the class was wrongly accused of some misdemeanour.

Despite gaining nine 'O' level GCEs and two 'A' levels, after leaving Cheltenham Grammar School Brian quickly ran through a succession of unskilled jobs, working at a record shop, an optician's, a sports shop, a factory and on the buses. (He retained an obsessive interest in buses, and later, when he could afford it, apparently took to buying double-deckers.)

Jones also gained a reputation for being an unprincipled Don Juan, leaving several illegitimate children in his wake.

Music appeared to be the sole outlet for his confused emotions, and therefore became the driving force in his life. It seems that at one point, fed up with work and with Cheltenham, he may have taken off for the Continent with his guitar and sax. Reputedly it was during this trip that he first encountered the blues, and also spent time improving on his guitar technique. Returning to Cheltenham, Brian joined a local band, The Ramrods, but was still frustrated by the absence of true American gutsiness in English jazz. His purchase of some difficult-to-come-by Elmore James records led him to buy a slide guitar, and to cultivate the James style – which Jagger and Richard recognized and admired at the Ealing club. Jones had put an ad in *Jazz News* in an attempt to find other musicians to play this type of music with him and Ian Stewart was one of those who replied. Brian had also been playing with Paul Pond – later Paul Jones of Manfred Mann.

Mike, Keith and Brian were all amazed to find others who shared their enthusiasms, and Jagger and Richard possibly chagrined to find someone their own age who was already a father. Keith remembers that at this point Jones was particularly interested in T-Bone Walker and jazz blues. Mike and Keith quickly introduced him to Jimmy Reed, Chuck Berry and Chicago blues he had never heard.

Soon Jagger and Richard took the stage themselves at Ealing. Encouraged by Cyril Davies, they did a Chuck Berry number, 'Around and Around'. The purist blues audience did not take to Keith's Chuck Berry-esque playing, though Jagger's singing had a dynamism that couldn't be ignored. Jagger claims that it was only this time, and on his debut at the Marquee, he has ever been nervous before performing.

It was the excitement of this first public performance that stimulated Mike Jagger to send a tape of five numbers, including 'La Bamba', 'Around and Around', 'Reelin' And

Rockin'', and 'Bright Lights, Big City', to Alexis Korner the following day, accompanied by a request to talk about further opportunities to perform. The enthusiasm was reciprocated; Cyril Davies had asked Korner to get hold of Jagger the same day.

After this Mike, like Brian, performed quite frequently with Blues Incorporated. Jagger's repertoire was at first severely limited; his three songs were Billy Boy Arnold's 'Poor Boy', 'Ride Em On Down', and 'Don't Stay Out All Night'. But the incomparable excitement of performing had bitten deep.

After three weeks of Korner's Saturday nights at Ealing, word had spread that something was happening. Harold Pendleton, manager of the Marquee Jazz Club in Wardour Street, Soho, who had a spare Thursday night slot to fill, went over to investigate. The music may not have been to his personal taste, but he was astute enough to spot something promising, and he confirmed with Korner the Thursday night slot at the Marquee for Blues Incorporated. Although their sounds were in contrast with the regular traditional jazz of the Marquee, the new Thursday spot soon found an audience of its own for its hard-hitting blues.

Mike Jagger was now forming a regular part of Blues Incorporated, singing in an uninhibited, physical style, and soon achieved his first press mention, in *Disc* for 19 May 1962:

SINGER JOINS KORNER
A nineteen-year-old Dartford rhythm and blues singer, Mick Jagger, has joined Alexis Korner's group, Blues Incorporated, and will sing with them regularly on their Saturday night dates at Ealing and Thursday sessions at the Marquee Jazz Club, London.

Jagger, at present completing a course at the London School of Economics, also plays harmonica.

This success might seem to have signalled the end of the

road for Little Boy Blue and the Blue Boys. Jagger was transformed by the chance to perform regularly in public.

But appearances were deceptive. In fact, since meeting Brian Jones, Keith had been playing with him regularly. Keith also went along to jam with the jazz band with which Brian was playing; they became the nucleus of a group. They were soon playing together two or three evenings a week, and chose a name, the Rolling Stones, after Muddy Waters' number 'Rolling Stone Blues'. Mick (no longer Mike) Jagger wanted to add the word 'Silver' to the title, an uncanny parallel with the Beatles, who tried out 'Silver Beatles' for a bit. But the 'Silver' was soon dropped in favour of the stronger, straight 'Rolling Stones' (or 'Rollin' Stones' for a very short period).

Gradually other members were drawn in: Ian Stewart, a pianist Brian had met playing boogie in a jazz club; Dick Taylor, still playing bass; occasionally Bob Beckwith from the Blue Boys. A purist blues guitarist, Geoff Bradford, soon departed after differences with Brian Jones. The Stones were short of a drummer, and tried to persuade Charlie Watts, who had been playing with Blues Incorporated, to join them, but with no success. They pulled in a Liverpool travelling salesman, Tony Chapman, as drummer. Jagger himself tended to be rather on the edge of things at first, since he was also busy with Blues Incorporated.

The group had taken to rehearsing in a cheap rented room over the Bricklayer's Arms pub in Broadwick Street, Soho – conveniently central for everyone to meet after work. (The pub has long since closed and been converted into a wholesaler's.) It wasn't long before Bob Beckwith dropped out to complete his education unhindered. The next job was to try to improve the group's equipment. Dick Taylor acquired a huge bass, Brian a new amplifier, and Mick's parents were magnanimous enough to donate a couple of Harmony amps.

Occasionally the Rolling Stones played as fill-ins for Alexis Korner at both Ealing and the Marquee, and they soon received their first approach from an optimistic agent. But their first public appearance in their own right came in July 1962, when Blues Incorporated were booked for a BBC TV date. Jagger was not required for the television show, which was going out live on a Thursday; the hitherto unknown Rolling Stones seized the chance and took over that Thursday's slot at the Marquee Club. So on Thursday 12 July 1962 Long John Baldry took the lead spot, and the Rolling Stones, consisting of Jagger, Richard, Jones, Dick Taylor, Ian Stewart and Mike Avery, played relief.

The Marquee gig earned them £20, and new admiration from Alexis Korner. They now started playing regularly at Ealing and the Marquee, and Mick began to think seriously about making music his career. Performing seemed to offer everything; what did a degree at the LSE and a straight career have to rival it? In *Jazz News* he said he hoped people wouldn't think they were a rock 'n' roll group; the rhythm and blues was their style. It wasn't long before Dick Taylor decided that education had to take priority, and dropped out of the band. He was later to reappear with the Pretty Things after a period at the Royal College of Art.

The time was right for the new group. The grip of jazz was loosening under the assault of rhythm and blues – the Beatles in Liverpool, the Animals in Manchester, and now the Rolling Stones in London. The Stones took the odd decision of joining the National Jazz Federation in an attempt to appease the old guard.

Keith, Brian and Mick moved into a flat in Chelsea in the summer. They seem almost to have gloried in its squalor. It consisted of a single room in a house in Edith Grove, in World's End. They eked out an existence on Mick's university grant, odd earnings, and food parcels from Keith's mother. They were looked after by some women from Liverpool ('four old whores . . . real old boots') in the flat below, and used to scavenge leftovers from parties in the teachers' flat upstairs. Their first 'manager', Giorgio

Gomelski, remembers discovering a foul-smelling glue bucket full of fag-ends, toilet paper, old socks and other rubbish in their flat. Somehow the bohemianism was *de rigueur*, a necessary apprenticeship for success, like the starving garret for the Romantic poet.

At quite an early stage the Stones visited Curly Clayton's tiny recording studio in Highbury and recorded three songs. Hopefully, they submitted the resulting tape to EMI, but with no luck. Brian had now taught himself to play the harmonica, but with Dick Taylor gone the Stones needed a new bass player. Tony Chapman introduced Bill Wyman at their Chelsea local, the Wetherby Arms in the King's Road. After playing an informal audition with them, he was invited to join the group, not least because he was the owner of a huge speaker and a large amplifier. Bill wasn't impressed with the band's name, but agreed to join there and then, having become disenchanted with the groups he was playing with at the time.

Bill Wyman contrasted sharply with the existing members of the band. Born on 24 October 1936, he was brought up in Penge, Surrey, but had been evacuated to Nottingham during the war. His parents were working class – his father a bricklayer, his mother a factory worker. The Perks family (Wyman is his stage name) encouraged music-making, and Bill could play the organ, piano and clarinet by the age of fourteen. He was a grammar school boy, and after Beckenham Grammar did an office job before National Service in the RAF. Bill married in October 1959, and the following year started his own group, the Cliftons.

With his wife and young child, working-class background, office job and neat appearance, the contrast is clear. Unlike the others, he was no rebel at school. 'I didn't kick up too much. There wasn't any point. If there was an argument going, I'd just try and look the other way.' He, too, early acquired a guitar and amplifier, and tried to make up for the tedious hours as a junior office boy by playing his guitar. Bill

Wyman has continued to be more self-contained, more private, than the other Stones. His personal life has been less publicized, his early collecting hobbies developing into his role of 'official' librarian of the Stones' archives. It is indicative of his strict division between work and private life that his home is said not to feature musical instruments, the tools of his trade.

One more member was needed before the Rolling Stones were complete. Tony Chapman's job of travelling salesman in the North of England made it impossible for him to remain a regular member of the group, and he eventually left to form a band called the Preachers. Charlie Watts, regular drummer with Blues Incorporated, had been pestered for months by Mick and Brian in an attempt to get him to join the Stones, but without success. They tried Mick Avery, later a member of the Kinks, and Carlo Little, and finally in desperation pulled in a jazz drummer called Steve Harris. He remembers that at this time the band was earning about £25 a night on their gigs.

Charlie Watts was still unsure about whether to join the Rolling Stones. He had completed his course at Harrow College of Art and was now working as a graphic designer with Charles Hobson & Gray, a Regent Street advertising agency. He was also playing in the evening at clubs like the Troubadour in Chelsea. Mick Jagger was still at the London School of Economics; Ian Stewart with ICI; why should Watts chuck in a secure job for the lottery of the music business?

Watts was born in Islington, North London, on 2 June 1941. His father was a lorry driver with British Railways. Charlie was given a £12 drum kit for Christmas when he was fourteen, and used to accompany jazz records with his own drumming. When he started playing with Blues Incorporated at the Ealing Club, the Stones were the only group there not getting paid – which did nothing to increase Watts' desire to join them. Still only nineteen, Charlie had a curiously middle-aged carefulness about him. Early pen portraits persist in talking about him as a 'smart, natty dresser'; these days he is reputed to take only one change of clothes even on the longest of tours. Another early obsession, with antique guns, was also noticed, together with an interest in the American Civil War.

Eventually, in January 1963, Charlie capitulated, working with the Rolling Stones in the evenings and pursuing his agency career during the day. Only a few months before he had been an out-and-out advocate of modern jazz; now he decided that R&B was the coming thing, and wanted to make sure he was part of it. Turning up to rehearsals in collar and tie from work, Charlie (like Bill Wyman) displayed a marked contrast with the squalor of Edith Grove.

With the group complete, the Rolling Stones were ready to go. They now consisted of Mick Jagger, Keith Richard, Brian Jones, Bill Wyman, Charlie Watts and Ian Stewart. They played a number of venues, with varying success. Though they were beginning to find an energy and drive all their own, their audiences were not always ready for what they had to offer. They secured a regular Monday night booking at the black Flamingo Club, despite a poor initial response, and played regularly at other London jazz clubs, with gigs roughly four times a week – all this without advertising, management or publicity.

Jagger recognized that the time for change had come. 'The trad boom was on the way out. Clubs which had specialized in straight traditional jazz were taking the pinch – lots of them were closing down, but fast. Or changing over to the sort of music that Alexis Korner had been pioneering. We knew, quite definitely, by going round the different clubs, that audiences were looking for something as an alternative – though most of them didn't really know what it should be.'

Many jazz players had simply taken to R&B for the sake of survival, and looked askance at electric guitars. They hoped R&B would be only a passing craze, and made life hard for groups like the Rolling Stones at the rock 'n' roll end of things.

2

Come On . . .

Suddenly everything started to happen.

The Stones ran into an experimental film-maker called Giorgio Gomelski. As exotic as Alexis Korner, he was the son of a Russian doctor and a Frenchwoman, had hitch-hiked round the world, organized the first Italian jazz festival, and introduced the English to jazz performers from Chicago (where he also lived for a time) as promoter of the National Blues and Jazz Festival. Gomelski was now running the Crawdaddy Club on Sundays at the Station Hotel, Richmond, thirty minutes out of central London. Until 1962 the club featured jazz bands but, influenced by events at Alexis Korner's gigs, Gomelski was now featuring the Dave Hunt Rhythm and Blues Band as his resident group.

Gomelski heard the Stones at the Red Lion, Sutton, and was impressed. He offered them advice and encouragement, and they started coming out to the Crawdaddy Club occasionally. They liked the younger, less hidebound audiences Gomelski was attracting. After making fantasy plans to supplant the Dave Hunt Band, the Stones suddenly heard that Hunt was in fact quitting the Crawdaddy for a better spot in town. They were on to Giorgio immediately, and were offered the Sunday afternoon session, at a minimum of £1.50 each per gig, or half the take, if that was greater.

Starting in February 1963, the Rolling Stones held down an

eight-month residency at the Crawdaddy Club, and their reputation spread. Gomelski was pleased enough:

> These boys were really very good. In fact, I had a verbal contract with them to be their manager – and that arrangement suited me fine. I worked as hard as I could for the boys for a number of reasons. First, they were doing a great job for my club – really lifting it from the doldrums. Second, they were playing a brand of music that appealed to me personally, and had fired me with an ambition to see it better appreciated here in Britain. And third, I was fed up with a lot of the insipid rubbish that was making the Top Twenty.

It was Gomelski who helped knock the group into shape. He had no doubt that Brian Jones was the main driving force behind the Stones at this point. Jones tried to extract a written contract out of Gomelski, and was soon talking grandiosely about moving in star circles.

After only a few weeks, queues were forming outside the Station Hotel long before the doors opened for the afternoon's session. A writer from the *Richmond & Twickenham Times* was despatched to investigate the outlandish goings-on, and reported back to suburbia that teenagers in extraordinary clothing, with long hair and scruffy appearance, were thronging to hear the 'drunk, dirty and drugged' Rolling Stones. He wrote of: 'Hair worn Piltdown style, brushed forward from the crown like the Beatles pop group . . . Save for the swaying forms of the group on the spotlit stage, the room is in darkness. A patch of light from the entrance doors catches the sweating dancers and those who are slumped on the floor where chairs have not been provided . . '

Although such accounts doubtless provoked a *frisson* of horror among the citizens of Richmond-upon-Thames, it also attracted the curious to the club – art students, local teenagers and the like. The Stones also achieved their first serious write-up in the musical press. Giorgio Gomelski persuaded

Peter Jones, a freelance with the *Record Mirror*, to come down and see for himself what was going on at the Crawdaddy Club. He was impressed enough to get a story commissioned by Norman Jopling, with photographs by Bill Williams. It was headlined THE ROLLING STONES — GENUINE R&B.

As the trad scene gradually subsides, promoters of all kinds of teen-beat entertainment heave a long sigh of relief that they have found something to take its place. It's rhythm-and-blues, of course. The number of R&B clubs that have suddenly sprung up is nothing short of fantastic . . .

At the Station Hotel, Kew Road, the hip kids throw themselves about to the new 'jungle music' like they never did in the more restrained days of trad.

And the combo they writhe and twist to is called the Rolling Stones. Maybe you heard of them — if you live far from London the odds are you haven't.

But by gad, you will! The Stones are destined to be the biggest group in the R&B scene — if that scene continues to flourish. Three months ago only fifty people turned up to see the group. Now promoter Gomelski has to close the doors at an early hour with over 500 fans crowding the hall.

Those fans quickly lose their inhibitions and themselves to the truly exciting music. Fact is that, unlike all the other R&B groups worthy of the name, the Rolling Stones have a definite visual appeal. They aren't like the jazz men who were doing trad a few months ago, and who had converted their act to keep up with the times. They are genuine R&B fanatics themselves and they sing and play in a way that one would have expected more from a coloured US group than a bunch of wild, exciting white boys who have the fans screaming and listening to them.

27

They can get the sound Bo Diddley gets — no mean achievement. The group themselves are all red-hot when it comes to the US beat disc. They know their R&B numbers inside out and have a repertoire of about eighty songs, most of them ones which real R&B fans know and love.

With such a write-up the Crawdaddy inevitably became compulsory for anyone who wanted to be where the scene was. David Bailey, Jean Shrimpton, Eric Clapton, the Beatles all put in appearances. Peter Jones of *Record Mirror* passed on the word to a young man in a hurry, Andrew Moog Oldham. Still only nineteen, Oldham had first appeared on the scene as Sandy Beach, a singer/compère, in 1961, but without success. He next tried the incredible name Chancery Laine, still with no luck. Oldham was an out-and-out mod; his clothes and whole style proclaimed it unmistakably. He had too, that hardness, elegance — 'modernism' — which defined the militant youth subculture. He had apparently also worked on promotions for Mary Quant, as a doorman at Ronnie Scott's, and as press agent for singer Mark Wynter. Brian Epstein hired him for five months to promote the Beatles' first album *Please Please Me*. He had been talking about setting up a management agency with Eric Easton, a 'bumbly old Northern agent', who currently managed the DJ Brian Matthew, and guitarist Bert Weedon. The two men went down to Richmond together on 28 April to see the Stones in action. The queues, the excitement, the music told them everything.

Oldham and Easton introduced themselves. They were impressed. Easton's comparison was with the Beatles: 'The beat was much the same, the guitars were well featured. Possibly you could say the overall sound was much the same . . . except that the Stones were much more down to earth. More basic.'

Brian Jones and Mick Jagger went to see Easton the

following day. They took up his offer of management, and Oldham bought back the demo tape recorded by the Rolling Stones at the IBC studios in Portland Place. He immediately started to set up a new session. He later commented: 'I was probably forty-eight hours ahead of the rest of the business in getting them.' (He also claimed that Easton reckoned Jagger couldn't sing.)

Eric Easton decided that he and Oldham would handle all aspects of the Rolling Stones' music themselves, cutting out the Artists and Repertoire (A&R) man. Under the title Impact Sound – Britain's first independent label – they were to control recording, production and packaging, and to sell the eventual product to a record company.

No time was lost in fixing up a recording session, and within a fortnight the Stones were at the Olympic Studios in Barnes for a three-hour session. Oldham now had to confess to them his own complete lack of technical experience – he had in fact never handled a recording session before. The Stones had decided to record the uncharacteristic and obscure Chuck Berry number 'Come On', which they reckoned was their best chance. Missing their live audience, they were nervous and anxious at the session. When the three hours were up the recording engineer, Roger Savage, asked Andrew Oldham what he intended to do about mixing the tapes. Oldham had no idea what he was talking about, and had to be treated to a simple explanation of recording techniques.

Oldham managed to sign up the Rolling Stones with Decca records. Fortunately he went to Dick Rowe, the legendary figure who had said 'No' to the Beatles, telling Brian Epstein that they had no future. Determined not to make the same mistake twice, Rowe was willing to agree to Oldham's unusual terms, which included complete control of the music, and ownership of the master recordings by the Rolling Stones. But Rowe refused to accept the poor quality tape made at Olympic Studios.

After three more recording sessions, at the Decca Studios in

West Hampstead, an acceptable version of 'Come On' was finally achieved, to be coupled with Willie Dixon's 'I Wanna Be Loved'. The Stones did a transformation job on the Chuck Berry original. They tightened it up, gave it a clipped rhythm, a taut bass line, added a key shift in the middle, and speeded it up. Probably for the only time, Jagger toned down the lyrics, from 'some stupid jerk' to 'some guy'.

The single was released by Decca on 7 June 1963, and Oldham managed to fix the Stones' first TV appearance for the same day, on the popular *Thank Your Lucky Stars* show. This was the cause of the first serious difference between the manager and his new group. He insisted that they should dress up smartly for the BBC, whereas they argued that their image demanded their normal, rather scruffy, appearance. Oldham told them they had to be prepared to compromise, and finally persuaded them to wear houndstooth check jackets with velvet half-collars. Even so, the press featured several 'disgusted of Tunbridge Wells' letters, protesting about the long hair, latent sexuality and generally disreputable nature of their act. (The TV producer helpfully suggested to Oldham that he should get rid of the singer with the thick lips.)

This was certainly the right sort of start for a group that was later to major on its perversity. But the single in fact lacked something of the gutsiness of the Stones' current live performances. Norman Jopling, writer of the vital *Record Mirror* article, criticized 'Come On': 'The disc doesn't sound like the Rolling Stones. It's good, punchy and commercial, but it's not the fanatical R&B that audiences wait hours to hear. Instead, it's a bluesy commercial group that should make the charts in a small way.'

He was right. By dint of planned buying, fans managed to push the single to number fifty in the charts, and it stayed in the Top Fifty for the next twelve weeks. It featured on Radio Luxembourg, and the Stones now made their first out-of-London appearance, at a gig in Middlesbrough. But the recording certainly was not typical of the group; Brian Jones apologised for it: 'Once we've made an impression, then we can try out our real rhythm and blues routines.' They had been playing less commercial Chuck Berry numbers down in Richmond, such as 'Bye Bye Johnny' and 'Down The Road'.

At this stage, Jagger seems to have felt only part way into the professional music world, as he revealed in an interview in the *New Musical Express*: 'I suppose you could say we've made some concessions, but we still play what we like. We consider ourselves professional amateurs. We still have the enthusiasm to treat the business as an enjoyable pastime, but also the professionalism to realize that you can't turn up late for dates.'

Oldham was astute enough to see that controversy as well as compromise would do the Stones' image no harm. He had coined the slogan, 'The Rolling Stones aren't another group – they're a way of life'. Already the length of their hair had become a symbol of their rebelliousness. With hindsight, Oldham claimed that it was music and sex that first hit him when he went to hear the Stones at the Crawdaddy Club. In any event, he now set about manufacturing and using little incidents to ensure constant press coverage. He began to realize that 'in just a few months the country would need an opposite to what the Beatles were doing . . . The Stones were that opposite . . . The way the media was running was that you could invite the Beatles in for tea but you wouldn't invite the Stones.' Mick Jagger persuaded Oldham that the Stones had appeared in suits on the stage for the last time. The notorious headlines started to appear: WOULD YOU LET YOUR DAUGHTER MARRY A ROLLING STONE? . . .

However, as yet the Rolling Stones had not really become a distinctive force. They soon built up a fan club identical to that of every other aspiring band; but they were not performing their own music. Their main difference was that their roots were in R & B rather than rock 'n' roll.

On 29 September the Rolling Stones embarked on their

first ever UK tour, with thirty dates around the country. Here was another totally new experience: the hassle of touring, travel, unfamiliar venues, unfriendly hotels. The Stones featured well down on the billing for the concerts, but were very excited to be on the same bill as Bo Diddley, the 'hip king of Rhythm and Blues', the Everly Brothers and, a late addition, Little Richard. They didn't pass up their chances; Keith Richard made sure he found out more about guitar technique from Don Peake, of the Everly Brothers. The Rolling Stones, slightly abashed to find themselves sharing a theatre with Bo Diddley, quietly dropped all his numbers from their own repertoire for the tour. They also saw the beginnings of fan hysteria, which later became a regular feature of their tours. At this stage it was mainly a matter of letters stolen from their car number plates and obsessive attention from adolescent girls. But they were also getting used to being constantly on the move, often sleeping in Ian Stewart's Volkswagen van. Meanwhile, back in London Andrew Oldham, as 'executive producer', was making crucial decisions about tracks for albums, and thus forming their image.

Towards the end of this first tour a follow-up single was released by Decca. The Stones had planned on making this Leiber and Stoller's 'Poison Ivy' backed by 'Fortune Teller', from an American blues album called *We Sing The Blues*. But this was cancelled, and the Beatles, who the Stones had already met, intervened to the advantage of the new band. (There was as yet no feeling that the Stones should be writing their own material.)

Lennon and McCartney were up in London to receive their Variety Club awards from Harold Wilson, and bumped into Andrew Oldham. They offered him a half-finished song for the Stones to record, and when he accepted it went back with him to the rehearsal rooms to polish off their composition, 'I Wanna Be Your Man'. Seizing the chance to link their names with the Beatles, the Stones recorded the number, and this time fortunately made less heavy weather of the recording session. Eric Easton, who produced the recording at the Kingsway Studios, commented: 'They were getting the hang of the recording business. Where they'd been on edge, nervy, in the first sessions, they were now beginning to relax . . . to get themselves in the mood when they could really reproduce the sort of stuff they did in the clubs.'

The resulting single was released on 1 November and immediately entered the Top Fifty. It soon climbed into the Top Twenty and remained there for ten weeks consecutively. *Disc* commented: 'This Lennon/McCartney number is a raucous, belting beater which is chanted at flat-out pace. The guitar sound is good and earthy and the whole production has an exciting on-the-spot quality.' The timing was immaculate; the Beatles were at their peak, with countless Number Ones in the charts, topping the bill at 'Sunday Night at the London Palladium' and stealing the show at the Royal Variety Performance.

The B-side of the single was 'Stoned', recorded on an earlier occasion. A mood song, they freely admitted it was an inversion of Booker T's 'Green Onions', with Brian Jones taking the lead on the harmonica.

Were they forsaking their ideals by going blatantly for a commercial success with the Lennon/McCartney track? Jagger said later that the Rolling Stones never intended to carry on singing the blues forever, they simply wanted to introduce them to a wider audience. At the start, he claimed, 'we were blues purists who liked ever so commercial things but never did them on stage because we were so horrible and so aware of being blues purists . . .'

Oldham and Easton backed up the single's release with a concerted press campaign. Gene Pitney was quoted in the *Daily Mirror*: 'When I first saw them I didn't know whether to say hello or bark. But then I got to know them. They're something; really something.' They also got coverage in the *Sunday Times* Magazine and on BBC TV's *Monitor,* and fan mail started to roll in by the sack.

A second tour was organized to keep the ball rolling. This time they took in the ballroom circuit, more used to trad jazz and light rock. The Stones took the opportunity to listen to some of the other bands, and to pick up new numbers. They also began playing more of the faster, up-tempo numbers which the punters could dance to. On this tour they ran into trouble more than once with rockers outraged at their music, their hair, or their appeal to the rockers' women.

Sexuality was gradually becoming a more explicit part of the Stones' stage act. Brian Jones had quickly recognized the sexual excitement aroused by their stage performances, and began to respond to the demands of his adolescent fans with rhythmic body movements. Mick Jagger came in on the act too, and started to wear tight jeans and develop thrusting pelvic movements as they played.

Although Ian Stewart played piano for the single 'I Wanna Be Your Man', he now switched from playing in public to acting as the Stones' road manager. He sold his employee's shares in ICI, where he worked in the export sales department, to buy a van to transport the group to gigs.

Early in 1963 Mick Jagger first met Chrissie Shrimpton, seventeen-year-old younger sister of the fashionable model Jean Shrimpton. She had seen Jagger playing with Blues Incorporated, and went to hear the Stones at the Crawdaddy Club. They began seeing each other regularly, and there was even talk of marriage. Jagger seems to have experienced a feeling of being torn between conventional middle-class behaviour and the exciting wild world of rock; between completing his course at the London School of Economics and plunging headlong into music.

Chrissie was responsible for a column in the fan magazine *Tiger Beat* entitled 'From London With Love', retailing gossip from the rock world. Her relationship with Mick was often stormy; she objected to his wanting her to 'disappear' when fans appeared. He thought it would damage his image for his fans to know he had a steady girlfriend.

34

3

Not Fade Away

In January 1964 the Rolling Stones released their first EP *The Rolling Stones*, which included 'You'd Better Move On', 'Poison Ivy', 'Money' and 'Bye Bye Johnny'. They were one of the first groups to recognize the potential of EP sales, and took full advantage of it. 'Bye Bye Johnny' was another Chuck Berry number, but it was probably Arthur Alexander's 'You Better Move On' that took the EP into the best-selling league. The pace and rawness of the Stones' version met an instant response from the fans; Jagger gave everything he'd got to the plaintive, heart-rending lyric. In 'Bye Bye Johnny' it was Keith Richard who impressed, with his mastery of a Chuck Berry style on the guitar. In contrast, their rendering of 'Money' was much less distinctive.

Early in the new year, the Rolling Stones were off on their third UK tour, this time at the top of the bill. Along with them went Dave Berry, the Swinging Blue Jeans, the Ronettes and Marty Wilde.

A further tour in February and March, with John Layton, Mike Sarne and Jet Harris, was timed to coincide with the release of their third single, 'Not Fade Away', an old Buddy Holly number, and already a hit for the Crickets. The success of this single, which took the Stones up as far as Number Three in the charts, was perhaps partly due to help in the studio from Gene Pitney and the legendary American recording manager Phil Spector. The Stones had struck up a friendly relationship with Pitney, and Jagger and Richard wrote a US hit for him, 'That Girl Belongs To Yesterday', though they were still not writing songs for their own band.

Jagger and Richards' arrangement of 'Not Fade Away' gave it a distinctive Bo Diddley-esque R & B drive. For the session Phil Spector played maraccas, and Ian Stewart (not Gene Pitney) played piano for 'Little by Little' on the B-side. Buddy Holly had originally recorded 'Not Fade Away' on the B-side of 'Oh Boy'; it had a disconcertingly abrupt style of lyric: 'A love for real not fade away'. Altering the musical style considerably, the Stones came up with a blend of staccato chords and wailing harmonica, with Jagger's raw voice over. The whole recording session, at the Regent Sound studio in Denmark Street, Soho, was produced by Phil Spector.

'Not Fade Away' was the Stones' best yet – a verdict endorsed by the musical press and the fans. This time the *New Musical Express* had no hesitation: 'It's a solo voice showcase, but the backing beat is quite fantastic, with handclaps and wailing harmonica adding to the effect. That fascinating plaintive quality peculiar to all Norman Petty/ Buddy Holly numbers is prominent, despite raucous treatment.'

'Not Fade Away' also spread the Stones' fame much wider. It took them into the US charts, and became a Number One hit in France. The time was right for their first album, released by Decca in April 1964. It immediately went to Number One in the LP charts, taking over from the Beatles, who had dominated unchallenged for weeks. The album sold 150,000 copies in the first fortnight, and is still regarded as a classic first album.

The album cover itself marked a bold new style; no hyped cover blurb, simply the disc number and a photograph of the group. The gamble paid off. The album opened with 'Route 66', a Chuck Berry number, played fast and furious. Willie Dixon's 'I Just Wanna Make Love To You', also played at full pelt, had been a hit for Muddy Waters. The Stones made Jimmy Reed's 'Honest I Do' into a blues-style number, while

'I Need You Baby' was in effect a version of Bo Diddley's 'Mona' taken at full speed. The instrumental 'Now I've Got A Witness' featured Ian Stewart on piano and organ. The help from Spector and Pitney was acknowledged in the number, subtitled 'Like Uncle Phil and Uncle Gene'. Side One finished with the B-side of 'Not Fade Away', 'Little By Little'.

The album's second side included 'I'm A King Bee', previously recorded by Slim Harpo, Berry's 'Carol', Jagger and Richard's own 'Tell Me', and 'Can I Get A Witness', popularized by Marvin Gaye. The short number 'You Can Make It If You Try' prefigured Jagger's taste for such emotional ballads and was followed by the novelty song 'Walking The Dog' by Rufus Thomas.

The album was recorded at the Regent Sound studios in Tin Pan Alley, and has a kind of naive arrogance that underlines its strength. The Stones never merely repeated other artists' versions; they made them their own. Every track was made to justify its inclusion. Nor did the Stones flinch from the sexual innuendo implicit in so many of the blues songs; Mick Jagger was already relishing the *doubles entendres* of the lyrics.

With the Beatles, the Stones revolutionized the concept of the album. Until now, albums had been totally under the control of the A&R man. Now the Stones demanded a greater say, recording their own backing and trying to ensure that all the material on an album was worthwhile, rather than simply filling it up with makeweights. For this reason, the length of time between their albums' releases tended to increase as they insisted on greater and greater care in their creation.

The album also reached Number One in the States, forming the best possible prepublicity for the Stones' first US tour, which included a booking at New York's famous Carnegie Hall. It was only the previous February that the Beatles had become the first ever rock group to appear at the venue. Now Oldham and Easton were trumping them, clearly implying that the Stones were every bit as good as the Beatles.

And Andrew Oldham's publicity was having its predicted effect; the *Daily Mirror* claimed: 'If ever the parents of Britain are almost united it must surely be in their general dislike of these shaggy-haired discoveries . . . They are the anti-parent symbol.'

The Stones were booked into a full US tour, including television coverage. In the event it was not a resounding success. It soon became clear that their reputation had not everywhere preceded them, and in San Antonio, Texas, for instance, an audience of 3000 in the 20,000 seat auditorium gave them the bird. Ed Sullivan refused to have them on his prestigious TV show as he was afraid of offending his middle-class audience. Instead the Rolling Stones appeared on Dean Martin's *Hollywood Palace* show, with Martin capitalizing on their rebel image, pleading at the commercial break: 'Don't go away. You wouldn't leave me alone with these Rolling Stones, would you?'

But for the Stones, America was a knockout experience; they were excited by the novelty and by the energy. But it took them time to overcome the comparatively minor response they encountered.

While in the States, the Stones took the opportunity to record at the famous Chess Record Company studios in Chicago, following such heroes as Muddy Waters, Chuck Berry and Bo Diddley. (They actually met Chuck Berry, Muddy Waters and Willie Dixon while in Chicago.) The Rolling Stones found the recording engineer Ron Malo particularly helpful.

Probably the best thing to come out of this first US trip were the recordings made at Chess Studios. Much of the heavy soul-influenced album *Out Of Our Heads* was recorded there. Their next single was 'It's All Over Now', in a version strikingly different from the Valentinos' original; it reflected their new confidence as a group. The B-side, 'Good Times, Bad Times' had been recorded in London before the US trip.

The US trip also marked the Stones' full acceptance into the 'swinging set'. While in New York they successfully invaded the world of Andy Warhol and Baby Jane, of Bob Dylan and Jerry Schatzburg. And it was becoming increasingly clear that for the public Mick Jagger *was* the Rolling Stones. In the early days, as Keith Richard recalls, it was Brian Jones who pulled the group together. His musicianship and his unquenchable desire for star status ensured that he was out in front. But now Jagger had begun to personify the defiant sexuality, the aggression, the louche hooliganism of the Rolling Stones' public image. Although the touring Stones had failed to take Middle America by storm, they had become the darlings of the radical chic of New York. And Dylan apparently introduced them to pot.

Back in London the adulation was more general. For the first time the Stones pushed the Beatles into second place in the *Record Mirror* pop poll. In May plans were announced for a film, to be scripted by Lionel Bart and directed by Clive Donner. It was later postponed, and never heard of again. Jagger now had to move frequently from flat to flat to avoid the constant invasions of young girl fans. Chrissie Shrimpton moved in with him, and apparently sided with Charlie Watts when he informed Mick that he wanted to get married to his girlfriend Shirley Field. Jagger said marriage was out for the Stones; Watts retaliated by marrying secretly at a registry office in Bradford.

The single 'It's All Over Now' was quickly followed by another EP, *Five By Five*. Keith recalls, 'Back in the old *Five by Five* days we used to go down to the local record stores, buy up a whole bunch of soul singles, sit down by the record player and learn 'em.' This EP catches brilliantly the Stones' spontaneity and energy, which had been helped by their experience at Chess studios. The EP started with 'If You Need Me', with Ian Stewart's Hammond organ sounds giving a 'sacred' note to things. Their own number 'Empty Heart' is followed by the instrumental number '2120 South Michigan Avenue'. 'Confessin' The Blues' had been recorded in the very same studio by Chuck Berry in 1960. Finally, 'Around And Around' achieved all the power and drive needed for a classic rock track.

In contrast with their experience in the States, in Britain live performances were now invariably followed by teenage hysteria. Their appearance on the popular TV show *Juke Box Jury*, on the other hand, was greeted with abuse from older viewers. They were deemed 'charmless', 'boorish', 'objectionable', 'rude', 'ill-mannered', and 'anthropoid'. When they visited Rediffusion's London studio in Kingsway for the popular *Ready, Steady Go!* programme they were mobbed, and needed heavy police protection. At the Winter Gardens, Blackpool, it took a police baton charge to disperse the destructive crowd. Keith Richard explained that some of the audience, mainly composed of drunken Glaswegians, kept spitting at him during the show, causing him to lose his temper and kick out at them. The fans invaded the stage, ripping down curtains and smashing equipment. The police helped build up the Stones' troublemaking image by pronouncing pompously: 'We shall advise the Winter Gardens authorities that they must not have the Rolling Stones again.'

Brian was high on audience hysteria. 'I feel the excitement of the audience come right through to me, communicating like mad. I feel that I'm thoroughly alive, like I've lived a long time in the space of just a few minutes . . . The wilder the audience, the more there is in it for us.'

Charlie Watts gave a more perceptive analysis of what was happening in an interview in *Disc*: 'Sure, there's a lot of screaming and that . . . They get excited, too, and so do we when we're playing to 'em. It's the atmosphere, you know. Gets all hot and sticky, and everybody's having a great time. Riot's the wrong word. Enthusiasm is more like it . . . The faints and the shovings only started happening regularly since the newspapers started writing about riots.'

In August the Rolling Stones broke into Europe for the first time. The chaos followed them. At a concert in The Hague the press picked up that two girls had their clothes torn off during the turmoil. After this the Stones had a date at the famous Olympia, Paris, notable for the large number of youths in the audience. Jagger and Richard played up to them, helping charge up the audience to violence. The auditorium was torn apart, and the fans ran riot in the surrounding streets, with the gendarmerie arresting some 150 of them.

By now Jagger was becoming increasingly aware of what was likely to happen, and of the potency of his act: 'I feel all this energy coming from an audience . . . I often want to smash the microphone up or something because I don't feel the same person on stage as I am normally . . . I entice the audience, of course I do. I do it every way I can think of . . . Of course what I'm doing is a sexual thing. I dance, and all dancing is a replacement for sex . . . My dancing is pretty basic sexually. What really upsets people is that I'm a man and not a woman.'

The pop columnist Maureen Cleave commented perceptively: 'With his outlandish personal appearance – his long hair, his huge mouth, his minute hips, his girlish face already a caricature, he came to mean all sorts of different things to different people. He was uncommunicative, unforthcoming, uncooperative; nobody knew anything about him; all he had to do was stand there for the theories to form.'

With renewed determination the Stones set out for a second US tour, and this time encountered teenage riots as well as adult comminations. The mayor of Milwaukee told radio listeners that the Stones' performance would be 'an immoral thing for teenagers to be able to exhibit themselves at'. The mayor of Cleveland stated that 'Such groups do not add to the community's culture and entertainment'.

On this visit, Ed Sullivan did invite them on his show, but lived to regret it when the teenage audience rioted. He mended his bridges with his respectable audience: 'I promise you they'll never be back on our show . . . I didn't see the group until the day before the broadcast. They were recommended to me by my scouts in London. I was shocked when I saw them.'

Sullivan had to eat his words. The Stones returned for several spots on his show in the next few years. While in America this time, the Stones fitted in recording sessions in Los Angeles in preparation for future albums. They were also filmed on the TAMI Awards TV show, along with the Beach Boys, Gerry and the Pacemakers, Chuck Berry, Billy J. Kramer and several other groups.

Their second US tour coincided with the Stones' first American hit single, 'Time Is On My Side', which was quickly overshadowed by their success with R&B veteran Willie Dixon's 'Little Red Rooster'. Released in November, this immediately soared to Number One in the NME charts. Both records reflected a return to the Stones' basic R&B style. 'Little Red Rooster' was a daring choice for a single, but exemplified the Stones' determination not to be moulded into just another pop band. They still regarded themselves as an R&B group; to release 'Little Red Rooster' was to present this distinctiveness to the public. But it was to be the last time they tried it with a straight blues song. 'Rooster' was backed by 'Off The Hook', a Jagger/Richard number.

The same month that 'Little Red Rooster' appeared, Mick Jagger was called to appear in court at Tettenhall, Staffordshire, to answer three driving charges. Not for the last time, there was an irony in hearing the voice of an establishment lawyer defending in measured tones the reputation of his rebel client:

They are not long-haired idiots but highly intelligent university men. The Duke of Marlborough had much longer hair than my client, and he won some famous battles. His hair was powdered, I think, because of fleas – my client has no fleas! The Emperor Caesar Augustus was another with rather long hair. He won many victories . . . This unhappy country suffers from a perennial disease called the balance of payments crisis and it needs every dollar it could earn. The Rolling Stones earn more dollars than many professional exporters.

Mick Jagger was fined £16.

The list of incidents now becomes endless: failures to turn up at recording sessions; backing out of parties; fines for urinating outside a petrol station; bans from hotels and restaurants for wearing the wrong clothes; prohibition by ATV; banned from British United Airways for mercilessly nagging a stewardess.

But 1964 ended on a high. The Stones came top of *Melody Maker*'s poll for Vocal Instrumental Groups, and 'Not Fade Away' was the year's top single. More quietly, Charlie Watts published a little tribute to his personal hero, Charlie 'Bird' Parker, *Ode To A High Flying Bird*. This had been a great year for the Stones. A total of fifty different tracks were released; only twenty-two days had not been spent working, on the road or in the studio.

4

Satisfaction

1965 was to become a whirlwind of tours. The reports of riots and mayhem become boring in their repetition, but need summarizing to remember the extraordinary pressure under which the Rolling Stones were now operating. During the year they went twice to Ireland, Scandinavia and the United States, and also toured Australia, New Zealand, Singapore, Hong Kong, Canada and Germany, as well as completing TV and live performance and recording commitments in the UK.

On 30 January the new album *The Rolling Stones No. 2* was released in Britain. It once more boasted a cover with only a photograph on it, and it included material recorded in London, Chicago and Los Angeles. It contains rather more soul-influenced R&B, and several Jagger/Richard tracks, but overall fails to keep up the promise of the first album. The opening number, 'Everybody Needs Somebody To Love', lasted almost five minutes, and was followed by Jerry Leiber's 'Down Home Girl' and Chuck Berry's 'You Can't Catch Me'. 'Time Is On My Side' had been rerecorded at Chess Studios; Mick Jagger was dissatisfied with their version on the American single, recorded in Regent Studios, Denmark Street. Side One finished with two more Jagger/Richard compositions: 'Heart Of Stone' and 'Grown Up Wrong'.

Side Two of the new album opened with 'Down The Road Apiece', another Chuck Berry number, with classy guitar work by Keith Richard. The folksy 'Under the Boardwalk' caused trouble at the recording sessions, and was followed on the album by Muddy Waters' 'I Can't Be Satisfied', with its Hawaiian-sounding guitars. Otis Redding's hit 'Pain in the Heart', a slow blues ballad, was followed by Jagger and Richard's lighthearted 'Off The Hook' and the short Dale Hawkins' song 'Susie-Q'. The album soon climbed to the top of the charts.

The Stones' Australian tour was made along with an odd team consisting of Roy Orbison, Rolf Harris and Dionne Warwick. There was the usual tumultuous welcome at Sydney Airport, the sellout concerts, and the press reports of scandalous happenings. When the papers reported that the Stones were spending their time at all-night parties, Mick rejoindered: 'We wish we were.'

The successful Australian trip was followed by the release of another single, 'The Last Time', backed by 'Play With Fire'. The title number was by Jagger and Richard – their first A-side composition – and they had recorded it in Los Angeles at the RCA Hollywood studios *en route* for Australia. Predictably, it went straight to the top of the charts. Recorded under the direction of Dave Hassinger, 'The Last Time' has an abrasive, discordant quality that adds to its memorability. It seems to herald heavy metal sounds, and is an attempt to marry Country & Western with R&B. 'Play With Fire' similarly prefigures the Stones' fascination with decadence, with its underlying masochistic themes. (Jagger and Richard were joined by Phil Spector and Jack Nitzsche for the early morning recording; Brian, Charlie and Bill had long since fallen asleep.) With the success of 'The Last Time', the Stones knew they were on the road with their own songs; they no longer had to rely on cover versions of other people's numbers.

That year's American tour was much more successful, and included a return visit to *The Ed Sullivan Show*. (The single 'Heart of Stone' had been released in January in the States, to a mixed reception.) Their concert at London, Ontario, was stopped when police turned off the stage power supply and switched on the house-lights after serious rioting. While the group was in New York, a television show entitled *Beatles v. Rolling Stones* was screened.

While in the States the Stones once more fitted in several useful recording sessions. Seventeen hours at Chess, Chicago, produced James Brown's 'Try Me', Otis Redding's 'That's How Strong My Love Is', and 'Mercy, Mercy' as well as Nanker/Phelge's 'I'm The Under Assistant West Coast Promotion Man', a cheeky tribute to George Sherlock, promoter with London Records.

At RCA, Hollywood, they recorded Otis Redding's 'I've Been Loving You Too Long', Sam Cooke's 'Good Times', Solomon Burke's 'Cry To Me', the Temptations' 'My Girl' and their own compositions 'The Spider And The Fly', 'One More Try' and '(I Can't Get No) Satisfaction'.

'Satisfaction' was first released in the States, had become the Stones' first American Number One hit and sold over 1,000,000 copies before it ever appeared in the UK. It was not only recorded and first released in America – it was also written there. Keith Richard first came up with the song in the form of a folk ballad, beside a swimming pool in Tampa, Florida, or so the story runs . . . 'Keith didn't like it much. He didn't think it would do very well . . . He was too close to it and just felt it was a silly kind of riff.' He claims it was based loosely on 'Dancing In The Streets' by Martha and the Vandellas, though its frustrated tone is totally in contrast to their song. It combines a blues-style lyric with a soul sound to make a classic rocker. 'Satisfaction' seems to define sixties rock, and is a quintessential riff song. With its driving energy, the lyric articulates the bored frustration of youth in a materialistic culture. More than anything else, it was probably this single, with its huge worldwide sales, that finally launched the Stones into their superstar status.

But the wild scenes continued as the tours succeeded one another. In Dublin the audience invaded the stage, assaulting everyone except Charlie Watts. In Denmark Brian was knocked unconscious by an electric shock from the equipment. In Belfast seats were smashed up and hurled onto the stage. In Germany seventy people were injured in the riots following the outrageous performance; the trouble was provoked largely by Jagger's goosestepping Nazi-style improvisation during 'Satisfaction'.

Only nine weeks after 'Satisfaction' came another single, 'Get Off Of My Cloud', which reached the Number One spot in the UK and the USA in the same week. The lyrics perhaps reflect the Stones' disorientation after a period of intensive touring; the chord sequence is only a marginal alteration to the Beatles' 'Twist And Shout', but the lyrics are distinctly Dylan-esque. The B-side, 'The Singer Not The Song' is a beat ballad, with a Beatles sound about it.

In June 1965 the live EP *Got Live If You Want It!* was released, including live performances previously released as studio-recorded tracks. Side Two finished with the popular 'I'm Alright' by Nanker/Phelge, with its mounting tension heightened by the audience screams. The tracks were recorded during March 1965 in Liverpool, Manchester and Greenford, during a UK tour.

On their fourth trip to the States the Stones were once more confounded by audience reactions. Now they were star celebrities in the States too, and expected to earn $1,500,000 gross. But the Americans were tending to treat them as Artists with a capital A. Jagger complained about 'this ridiculous sort of intellectual approach towards the group'. In an extraordinary bit of publicity, a hundred-foot illuminated picture of the Stones was erected in New York's Times Square, with a bit of nonsense written by Andrew Oldham: 'The sound, face and mind of today is more relative to the hope of tomorrow and the reality of destruction than the blind who cannot see their children for fear and division. Something that grew and related, five reflections of today's children . . . the Rolling Stones.'

But there were already signs of destruction beneath the

apparently unstoppable success. Brian Jones was increasingly disturbed about his own role within the group. In many ways the original instigator of the Rolling Stones, and their early leader, he resented Mick Jagger's takeover as leader and symbol of the band. More and more people were talking about 'Mick Jagger and the Rolling Stones', a constant needle to Jones. Jagger later commented: 'Even though we were all working together, Brian desperately wanted to be the leader, but nobody ever accepted him as such . . . Up until then it was accepted by the public that the singer with the band was the leader and, as I just happened to be the singer, most people automatically singled me out as the leader.'

For Jones it also rankled that Jagger and Richard were writing all the group's songs, despite the fact that both Jones and Bill Wyman could write. Although his resentment was beginning to make itself felt, there was certainly no suggestion that he should leave the group. For one thing, his musicianship was simply too valuable. As performer on a range of instruments – guitar, dulcimer, mellotron, organ, harmonica – he was not expendable.

Listening to the early singles, Jones' contribution is obvious. In 'The Last Time', his guitar supplies both rhythmic impulse and harmonic fill-in. On 'Money' and 'Come On', his mouth organ provides the characteristic reedy key-note, but never threatens to take over in a selfish virtuoso performance. His skill at the mellotron transforms 'Play With Fire' into a 'pop masterpiece', a sort of downbeat ballad.

But Mick Jagger was certainly being singled out for the lionizing both by fashionable society and by the gossip press. Cecil Beaton painted him, he was best man at fashionable photographer David Bailey's wedding, guest at the twenty-first birthday celebrations for the Guinness heiress.

With the money now pouring in, the Stones decided it was time for a change in management. Oldham and Jagger wanted to go with Allen Klein, who had risen to success in New York. The London manager Mickey Most signed up

Klein for most of his groups, and this brash figure became a major force in the British rock scene. In the spring of 1965 Oldham took on Allen Klein as his own financial manager.

Eric Easton's contract came up for renewal the same year, and the Stones sacked him in favour of Klein, who became their business manager. Andrew Oldham continued to act as manager, and Tito Burns became their new agent. Klein immediately renegotiated terms with Decca, emerging with advances on royalties totalling £2,800,000, probably the most valuable single recording contract ever.

This all left the group – and particularly the songwriting team of Jagger and Richard – very rich. Jagger had no qualms: 'I came into music just because I wanted the bread . . . I looked around and this seemed to be the only way to make the kind of bread I wanted. It worked, and I don't treat it as a joke. It's my business.'

In the summer of 1965 the new album *Out Of Our Heads* was released. Opening with the up-tempo 'She Said Yeah', Otis Redding's 'Mercy, Mercy', with a heavy blues feel, and 'Hitch Hike' with Brian Jones in top form, the album continues with another Redding number, 'That's How Strong My Love Is', featuring a great climax, Sam Cooke's 'Good Times' and the Jagger/Richard composition 'Gotta Get Away'.

Side Two starts with Chuck Berry's 'Talking 'Bout You', with a splendid guitar break, Jagger's version of Solomon Burke's 'Cry To Me', 'Oh Baby (We Got A Good Thing Going)' and Jagger/Richard numbers 'Heart of Stone', 'The Under Assistant West Coast Promotion Man' and 'I'm Free'.

Out Of Our Heads was their first all-American recorded album, and displays a greater technical sophistication. Jagger's singing has evolved into something distinctly more assured, and the Stones' own numbers are delivered without a trace of apology.

1966 was distinctly inconclusive. It was a year of transition, and of coming to terms with superstardom and its perils. There was yet another American tour, a trip to Australia and New Zealand, and tours of Belgium, Holland, France, Germany, Sweden and Denmark. In Marseilles Mick Jagger was hit by a chair thrown from the audience, and in Paris a smoke bomb landed on the stage.

Just before their fifth tour of North America, which comprised twenty-eight cities in thirty-six days, Jagger himself collapsed from nervous exhaustion. He was ordered to rest for a fortnight. Some sceptics suggested it was drugs that precipitated the collapse.

Ironically, the single '19th Nervous Breakdown', released on 4 February, immediately won a Gold Disc. Fittingly, it had been recorded at five in the morning. It amounted to a putdown of spoilt upper-class women, and included the first unmistakable drug reference in a Stones' song. '19th Nervous Breakdown' was backed by 'As Tears Go By', originally recorded by Marianne Faithfull. The Stones ran it slower, and added a string quartet and acoustic guitar.

The next single was the rather dark and mysterious song 'Paint It Black', about a girlfriend's death and funeral. 'Paint It Black' in fact started out as a mickey-taking session on Eric Easton, one-time electronic organist. Jack Nitzsche added a gypsy-style piano backing, Brian an innovative sitar. The B-side, 'Long Long While', was a fine soul ballad of the Otis Redding school.

In September came 'Have You Seen Your Mother, Baby?', promoted with a deliberately shocking photograph of the group in a New York street dressed in drag and heavy make-up. Jagger was dressed as a black granny, Brian as a Jean Harlow blonde, and Bill Wyman as a US servicewoman. Jagger described it all as 'a bit of a giggle', but later suggested that events had begun to run away with them and this was 'the ultimate freak-out. We came to a full stop after that'.

The new album, *Aftermath*, was released in June 1966. It had been held up for weeks when Decca refused to release it under its intended title *Could You Walk On Water?* 'We would not issue it with *that* title for any price.'

The LP opened with 'Mother's Little Helper', with its bouncy rhythm and Brian's sitar accompaniment. In contrast to this was 'Stupid Girl', with a pounding beat and great guitar break by Keith. 'Lady Jane', a slow ballad, as romantic as the Stones could be, had Brian on dulcimer and Jack Nitzsche on harpsichord. The macho 'Under My Thumb' had Keith Richard dubbing over an extra bass, and Brian Jones on marimbas; it was followed by a very pacey 'Doncha Bother Me'. The final track on Side One was 'Goin' Home', which lasted eleven and a half minutes, the band playing a fade-out of over eight minutes on the number.

On Side Two, 'Flight 505' featured a honky-tonk piano and Berry-esque guitar; 'High And Dry' had a distinctly Country & Western feel to it, with Keith Richard on twelve-string guitar. It was followed by 'Out Of Time', 'It's Not Easy', with Jagger's fine vocal, and the folksy 'I Am Waiting'. Then 'Take It Or Leave It', 'Think', with a great guitar break, and finally, 'What To Do'.

The album was their first to feature solely Jagger/Richards numbers, and their first to use the sitar. It was produced at the RCA Victor Studios in Hollywood by Dave Hassinger, and quickly achieved Number One position in the charts. It has another first: it lays bare for the first time the Stones' blatant male chauvinism, reflecting sex as an easy come, easy go commodity. Women are dismissed as pretty mindless: 'She's the worst thing in the world' ('Stupid Girl'); 'She does just what she's told' ('Under My Thumb'); 'You're obsolete my baby' ('Out Of Time').

Though this album was frequently compared with the Beatles' *Rubber Soul*, it is totally the Stones'. It has some of Jagger's most idiosyncratic lyrics, and explores a wide range of instrumental sounds. The vituperation and vindictiveness are unmistakable, and underline the anti-romantic realism that the Stones had borrowed from R&B.

Later in the year a Greatest Hits album, *Big Hits (High*

Tide And Green Grass) was released, with less than total success.

The touring continued that year (1966), but the Stones were beginning to receive a little wary respect from official-dom, which was nonetheless still agitated about the threat to property. Now they were banned from hotels not because of their own behaviour or appearance but for fear of the harm the fans would wreak in their wake. In New York they were accommodated in a yacht for safety and inaccessibility. In Boston tear gas was used to disperse the rioting audience; in Montreal thirty huge bouncers were hired by the manage-ment to deal with unruly fans, to the alarm and annoyance of the Stones, who stopped playing in protest. Andrew Oldham stirred up publicity by putting out a story that the Stones were suing fourteen New York hotels for damages totalling $5,000,000 for refusing the group accommodation.

By now the Stones had acquired a status all their own. The opening of their 1966 UK tour – their last for four years – was the major event of the music world. It was held at London's Royal Albert Hall; among the audience were Keith Moon of the Who, Jonathan King, and ex-yardbird Paul Samwell-Smith. There was the normal mayhem on stage: Keith Richard was knocked to the floor, Mick was almost throt-tled, and Brian and Bill fled. Only when the management threatened to cancel the show did the audience return to their seats. Then,

> Mick – dressed in an orange shirt, white bell-bottomed trousers and black sequined Chinese-style jacket – ran forward and started with 'Paint It Black'. Charlie then walked to the front of the stage and announced 'Lady Jane' . . . Brian, looking elegant in grey trousers, purple velvet jacket and silk shirt and white cravat sat down to play an instrument resembling an electric zither. 'Not Fade Away', 'The Last Time'. 'Have You Seen Your Mother, Baby?', 'Standing In The Shadow' followed before they closed with 'Satisfaction'.

Somehow the seriousness with which they were now being taken began to make the Stones take themselves more seriously. They were beginning to believe their own publicity. In a *New Musical Express* interview Brian Jones came up with an extraordinary ragbag of opinionated views:

Our generation is growing up with us and they believe in the same things we do ... our real followers have moved with us – some of those that we like most are the hippies in New York, but nearly all of them think like us and are questioning some of the basic immoralities which are tolerated in present-day society – the war in Vietnam, persecution of homosexuals, illegality of abortion, drug taking. All these things are immoral. We are making our own statement – others are making more intellectual ones. Our friends are questioning the wisdom of an almost blind acceptance of religion compared with total disregard for reports related to things like unidentified flying objects which seem more real to me. Conversely I don't underestimate the power or influence of those, unlike me, who do believe in God. We believe there can be no evolution without revolution. I realize there are other inequalities – the ratio between affluence and reward for work done is all wrong. I know I earn too much but I'm still young and there's something spiteful inside me which makes me want to hold on to what I've got. I believe we are moving towards a new age in ideas and events. Astrologically we are at the end of the age called Pisces – at the beginning of which people like Christ were born. We are soon to begin the age of Aquarius, in which events as important as those at the beginning of Pisces are likely to happen.

But Brian's difficulties within the group were beginning to worsen. With Jagger and Richard busy writing, Brian would go out and meet the celebrities, returning unfit for the next day's session. So began the habit of overdubbing his parts, and increasingly it was not the whole band playing numbers . recorded.

It was Andrew Oldham who pushed Keith and Mick into writing songs together seriously. Keith claims that Andrew locked him and Mick Jagger into the kitchen for two nights, until they came out with a song. Emulating the Beatles, they formed their own music publishing company, and were now beginning to see the possibilities for using their own songs in recordings and concerts. Their first album had included the Jagger/Richard number 'Tell Me', and two pseudonymous numbers, under the name Nanker/Phelge, a private joke. (Nanker was from their word 'Nankies', meaning little men representing authority. 'We take them off by pulling down the underneath of our eyes and pushing up the end of the nose.' Jimmy Phelge was a printer of unsavoury habits who once shared a flat with some of the Rolling Stones.)

To their own disgust most of their early writing took the form of rather sentimental romantic ballads. It was for this reason that they gave them to other artists, such as Gene Pitney, to sing; they didn't fit the Stones' aggressive image. They wrote a number of songs for fellow artists: 'Blue Turns To Grey' for Cliff Richard, 'Sittin' On A Fence' for Twice As Much, and 'Out of Time' for Chris Farlowe, as well as 'As Tears Go By' for Marianne Faithfull.

Within the writing team it was generally Jagger who supplied the lyrics, Richard the music, at least at first. Later the division of labour became less clear, and neither of them was willing to analyse the process particularly carefully. Keith Richard claims that 'The Last Time' was the first of their compositions he really liked; Andrew Oldham was anxious for them to produce more pop-oriented songs, while Jagger and Richard began gradually to come up with soul-influenced numbers.

Mick Jagger's relationship with Chrissie Shrimpton continued along a rocky course. She claims that his habit of

54

asking her to disappear when fans were in evidence, and his increasingly wild behaviour, made her feel more and more insecure. Though he talked about marriage, nothing came of it, and Chrissie became disenchanted with aspects of the pop scene. She resigned herself to the fact that Mick was unprepared for marriage at this point.

Mick Jagger first met Marianne Faithfull back in 1964. Still only seventeen, she was striking, with her long blonde hair and innocent, delicate features. She was with her boyfriend John Dunbar; Andrew Oldham promptly arranged to record her, though he had never heard her sing a note. She recorded Jagger and Richard's number 'As Tears Go By', discarded as too sentimental for the Stones themselves; it was issued as the A-side of her first single.

By 1966 Jagger's relationship with Chrissie was coming to an end. He commented: 'Three years is a long time to be with someone.' He began to see much more of Marianne Faithfull, though she was still involved with Dunbar, whom she married.

5

Their Satanic Majesties

In January 1967 the Rolling Stones issued their fifth album, *Between The Buttons*, and their twelfth single, the double A-side 'Let's Spend The Night Together'/'Ruby Tuesday'. The single immediately caused trouble; it may have been the late sixties, but there were still howls of protest about this alleged incitement to teenage promiscuity. (In fact the lyrics were considerably more subversive than the title line suggested, as David Bowie's later version revealed.) Underground rumour also claimed that Ruby Tuesday was one of the livelier groupies on the scene.

Ed Sullivan was demurring once again: unless the title line was changed for their live performance, the Rolling Stones could not appear on his show to plug their single. Fans accused Jagger of selling out when he appeared as billed on Sullivan's US television show, and seemed to sing 'Let's spend *some time* together'. Compromise! Jagger claimed later that he mumbled across the controversial words; but that was hardly less of a climb-down. Later he said he was sorry that he had failed to stand firm and hadn't simply walked out on the show.

Between The Buttons boasted an album sleeve featuring drawings by Charlie Watts. Side One opened with 'Yesterday's Papers', with original background effects including chime-bells and plenty of bass pedal. 'My Obsession' had a strong boogie-woogie piano and a stretched bass effect. 'Back Street

Girl' built up a French flavour, with its accordion and tambourine backing. Next came the very speedy 'Connection', 'She Smiled Sweetly' with prominently featured organ, and a finale 'Cool, Calm and Collected'.

After 'All Sold Out', Side Two continued with the Diddley-esque 'Please Go Home', the Dylan-esque 'Who's Been Sleeping Here?', with its harmonica and acoustic guitar, and the fast rocker 'Miss Amanda Jones'. The side finished with a five-minute instrumental jamboree. But the album failed to match their previous LPs; the Stones were in some ways marking time. It was from this album onwards that it was no longer accurate to say that Jagger wrote the words, Richard the music. There was often a more complex collaboration, with Jagger also suggesting tunes and Richard contributing to the lyrics.

A few days after the Ed Sullivan contretemps the Stones were once more at the centre of a trivial controversy in England. They appeared on the nationwide television show *Sunday Night At The London Palladium* to plug 'Let's Spend The Night Together', miming to the pre-recorded track. But they refused to appear on the famous roundabout with their fellow guests at the customary end-of-show farewell. The disagreement rapidly mushroomed into a tabloid sensation, and was revived by Terry Scott, the comedian, on the Eamonn Andrews show a fortnight later. Meanwhile a photograph of Brian Jones in Nazi uniform, with a doll beneath one jack-booted foot, appeared in the British press, and provoked an understandable outcry. And Bill Wyman's seven-year marriage finally broke up.

The Stones were certainly starting the year controversially. On Sunday 5 February the *News Of The World*, in a feature on pop stars and drugs, named Mick Jagger among those involved. (This was in fact the result of mistaken identity; Brian Jones had been heard advocating drugs; he was subsequently quoted as 'Mick Jagger'.) Jagger quickly denied the allegations, and talked of a libel action against the newspaper.

The following Sunday, 12 February, at 8.05 p.m., Keith Richard's country house Redlands, in Sussex, was raided by police. They had evidently received a tip-off. They found the Stones and a number of friends and acquaintances at a party. Marianne Faithfull, who had been out for a walk, was wrapped only in a rug.

The raid itself amounted to a confrontation between two cultures, all conducted amid the aroma of joss-sticks and with Dylan's voice pounding from a record player. There was a certain selectivity or amateurishness about the police search; one case filled with chemicals was quickly dismissed when its owner stated it contained only unprocessed film. On Mick Jagger the police discovered four pep-pills he had bought legally in Italy as an antidote to airsickness.

Jagger, Richard and a friend named Robert Fraser were all subsequently summonsed to a hearing on 10 May. As their lawyer commented: 'They really want to do it to you'. This was undoubtedly true. Brian Jones in particular had been notably less than prudent in his use of pills.

Brian had met the German film actress Anita Pallenberg in 1965. He steadily went deeper and deeper into the drug culture, and his habit probably helped precipitate the breakdown he suffered, and for which he spent a period in Switzerland to recuperate. Anita left Brian in favour of Keith Richard, leaving him feeling still more isolated and disorientated.

The Stones were unclear about who had tipped off the police to make the Redlands raid. Accusing fingers pointed at a man called Robert Schneidermann, who had been at the Redlands party but escaped unscathed, and shortly afterwards left the country.

Under the shadow of the forthcoming court appearances the group left for their first European tour in twelve months, a tour that included dates in Eastern Europe. As usual, rioting followed them. There were 150 arrests in Vienna, truncheon-wielding police in Stockholm, tear-gas and water-cannon in Warsaw. But now the Stones faced a new problem: thorough searches of their luggage every time they went through a customs post. They had evidently been put on some international drugs blacklist.

Jagger began to foresee trouble: 'Teenagers the world over are weary of being pushed around by half-witted politicians who attempt to dominate their way of thinking and set a code of living . . . This is a protest against the system. And I see a lot of trouble coming in the dawn.'

The Stones now worked hard to record material for their next album, before the court hearing intervened. But by now Brian was regularly incapacitated by drugs; he would spend recording sessions lying on the floor while the others played in for him. But it wasn't solely the drugs and his sense of personal desperation – it was also Jones' opposition to the type of music for the forthcoming album – *Their Satanic Majesties*.

At the preliminary court hearing at Chichester on 10 May the three accused were all sent for trial: Jagger for illegal possession of four tablets of amphetamines; Richard for allowing his house to be used for the taking of drugs; and Robert Fraser for illegally possessing heroin. At the very time Jagger and Richard were appearing in the Chichester courtroom, the Chelsea drugs squad was raiding Brian Jones' London flat. They arrested him for possession of illegal drugs.

The Stones had by this time become a symbol of defiant hedonism, of decadence. There had been covert allusions to drugs in 'Satisfaction' and in '19th Nervous Breakdown'. These references were less carefully concealed in such numbers as 'Connection', 'Something Happened To Me Yesterday' and 'Paint It Black'.

The drugs trial opened on 27 June 1967, and Jagger and Richard, probably fearing little more than a deterrent fine, appeared in their customary stylish clothes. Mick Jagger was first to be called, to face the amphetamines charge. His doctor's evidence that the pills were in effect prescribed for him for emergency use was summarily dismissed by the judge, Leslie Block. The jury then took a mere five minutes to find Jagger guilty; he was remanded in custody to await sentence.

It was now Keith Richard's turn. His defence was that he did not know that drugs were being taken, and that the raid had been instigated by the *News of the World* to defeat the libel action that Jagger had threatened against the paper. He cited the fact that Schneidermann, present during the raid, had since left the country. It was during Richard's trial that the prosecution focused attention on the presence of the 'naked girl', attempting to suggest that she was high on drugs. WPC Fuller said in evidence:

> She was naked, apart from a fur rug wrapped round her, and in a merry mood. A policeman was standing at the top of the stairs. She said: 'They want to search me', and let the rug drop. She had nothing on. 'Miss X' seemed completely unconcerned about what was going on around her.

Counsel for the prosecution Malcolm Morris QC stressed the decadence of the scene at Redlands.

> There was a strong, sweet, unusual smell . . . That smell could not fail to have been noticed by Keith Richard. There was ash – resulting from cannabis resin and smoking Indian hemp – actually found on the table in front of the fireplace in the drawing room where Keith Richard and his friends were. The behaviour of one of the guests may suggest that she was under the influence of smoking cannabis resin in a way Richard could not fail to notice . . .
>
> All she was wearing was a light-coloured fur skin rug which from time to time she allowed to fall disclosing her nude body. She was unperturbed and apparently enjoying the situation.

Keith Richard, too, was duly convicted, but the real shock came when Justice Block delivered sentence. He pronounced a sentence of one year's imprisonment plus £500 costs on

Keith Richard; three months' imprisonment with £100 costs on Jagger. They were stunned. Fans were particularly shocked to see photographs of the pair in handcuffs.

It seemed like society's revenge. This was the way to control the rebels, the anarchic young. This was the way to put a stop to the apparently endless hedonism – a severe dose of jail. The Stones had in a way become victims of their own press hype: they had created themselves monsters in the eyes of the public, and were now being punished in the way society prescribed for monsters. Jagger had threatened society with his songs about drugs, freedom and sexuality; now society was hitting back.

After spending a couple of days in Brixton and Wormwood Scrubs respectively, Jagger and Richard were released on £17,000 bail pending appeal.

The following Saturday William Rees-Mogg, Editor of *The Times*, wrote a long leader entitled WHO BREAKS A BUTTERFLY ON A WHEEL? He questioned the punitive sentences passed on Jagger and Richard:

> . . . We have therefore a conviction against Mr Jagger purely on the ground that he possessed four Italian pep-pills, quite legally bought though not legally imported without a prescription . . .
>
> Mr Jagger's career is obviously one that does involve great personal strain and exhaustion; his doctor says that he approved the occasional use of these drugs, and it seems likely that similar drugs would have been prescribed if there was a need for them. Millions of similar drugs are prescribed in Britain every year, and for a variety of conditions.
>
> One has to ask, therefore, how it is that this technical offence, divorced as it must be from other people's offences, was thought to deserve the penalty of imprisonment. In the courts at large it is most uncommon for imprisonment to be imposed on first offenders when the

drugs are not major drugs of addiction and there is no question of drug traffic.

The normal penalty is probation, and the purpose of probation is to encourage the offender to develop his career and to avoid the drug risks in the future . . . It would be wrong to speculate on the Judge's reasons, which we do not know. It is, however, possible to consider the public reaction. There are many people who take a primitive view of the matter, what one might call a pre-legal view of the matter. They consider that Mr Jagger has 'got what was coming to him'. They resent the anarchic quality of the Rolling Stones' performances, dislike their songs, dislike their influence on teenagers and broadly suspect them of decadence . . .

As a sociological concern, this may be reasonable enough, and at an emotional level, it is very understandable, but it has nothing at all to do with the case. One has to ask a different question: Has Mr Jagger received the same treatment as he would have received if he had not been a famous figure, with all the criticism and resentment his celebrity has aroused? . . .

If we are going to make any case a symbol of the conflict between the sound traditional values of Britain and the new hedonism, then we must be sure that the sound traditional values include those of tolerance and equity.

It should be the particular quality of British justice to ensure that Mr Jagger is treated exactly the same as anyone else, no better and no worse.

There must remain a suspicion in this case that Mr Jagger received a more severe sentence than would have been thought proper for any purely anonymous young man.

Melody Maker sent *The Times* an ironic message: 'Keep on swinging!'

The next day the Sunday papers joined in. The *Sunday Times* detected a 'strong sour smell of ignorance', and commented that it was a 'show trial in which the prurient press coverage played an essential and predictable role. Because of the publicity, the decision on their sentences grew into a critical expression of public policy.' The *Observer* detected, 'The case has produced two martyrs'. The *News of the World* admitted it had received information that a drug party was taking place at Redlands on the evening in question, but categorically denied any connection with, or knowledge of, the mystery figure of Schneidermann, whom Richard alleged had set the whole thing up.

The appeal was heard at the end of July. Keith Richard's conviction was quashed: some of the evidence, particularly about the naked Miss X, was inadmissible. In Jagger's case, though a technical offence had been committed, 'There were only four tablets . . . no evidence of over-indulgence, peddling to others . . . the evidence of the doctor was the strongest mitigation there could be.' He was a given a conditional discharge.

Despite this, the Lord Chief Justice, Lord Parker, could not resist telling Jagger that his position laid him open to higher punishments: '. . . when one is dealing with somebody who has great responsibilities, as you have . . . if you do come to be punished it is only natural that those responsibilities should carry a higher penalty.' Jagger disagreed. He simply asked for his private life to be his own.

Brian Jones' case followed a similar pattern. His psychiatrist gave evidence that 'Any confinement in prison would completely destroy Brian Jones's health. He would go into a psychotic depression . . . and might well attempt to injure himself.' Jones was remanded on bail after the magistrates' court hearing; at the subsequent trial he was found guilty of possessing cannabis and sentenced to nine months' imprisonment. He was sent to Wormwood Scrubs, released on bail pending appeal, and finally his sentence was amended to a £1000 fine, three years' probation and statutory medical attention.

Following his release, Mick Jagger participated in a grandiose media event set up by ITV. He was to confront Lord Stow Hill, the controversial Bishop of Woolwich, Father Thomas Corbishley and the Editor of *The Times* in a debate about the younger generation for the current affairs programme *World In Action*. It was all very pretentious, and symbolized the Stones' extraordinary status in the Britain of the late sixties. Suddenly it appeared that their music was in a way less important than their status, their significance as representatives of a new, free generation. Rock now represented a form of high culture, and the Stones were priests of that cult. The shivers that passed through the younger generation when the photographs of the handcuffed Jagger and Richard appeared in the press were unmistakable.

Mick Jagger claimed that the whole episode seriously frightened him. 'I hated the bust because I felt it stopped the band and slowed it down. I think being busted still *does* slow the band down . . .'

The release of Jagger and Richard was followed shortly by the new single 'We Love You'/'Dandelion', which capitalized on the prison experience with the sounds of clanking cell doors. The single was described as a thank you to those who supported the Stones during the court hearings. This was the summer of Flower Power – of long hair and tinkling bells, psychedelic shirts and beads. The Rolling Stones also made a promotional film that included dramatized scenes from the trials of Oscar Wilde, with its obvious parallels in their own experience.

This new single was the Stones' answer to 'All You Need Is Love' – but it didn't match up, although Lennon and McCartney sang the backing harmonies. It never reached higher than eight in the charts.

Mick Jagger and the Rolling Stones never really got into transcendental meditation and the great wave of psychedelia in a big way. Jagger warned people not to take 'We Love You' seriously. 'It's just a bit of fun . . . I'm not involved in

The Rolling Stones – an early photo-call. *Left to right:* Charlie Watts, Bill Wyman, Mick Jagger, Brian Jones and Keith Richard.

The Rolling Stones 1978 line-up. *Left to right:* Keith Richard, Charlie Watts, Ron Wood, Mick Jagger, Bill Wyman

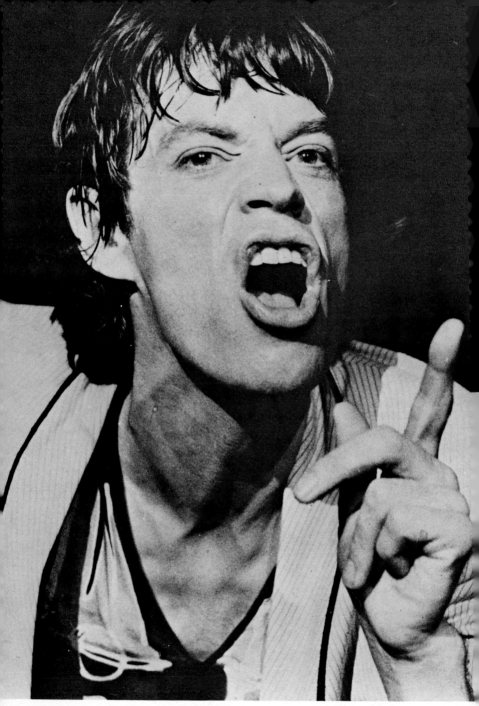

Mick Jagger

this "love and flowers" scene, but it is something to bring people together for the summer.' Mick and Marianne had the compulsory meeting with the Maharishi, and left it at that – apart from the uniform of exotic bright clothing.

Work began on *Their Satanic Majesties Request* (released in December 1967) as long ago as late 1966. In some ways the album was the result of the Rolling Stones' feeling that they were coming off second best in public comparisons with the Beatles. To add to this fear, Dylan had informed Keith Richard: 'I could have written "Satisfaction", but you cats could never have written "Tambourine Man".' In April 1967 the Beatles released *Sergeant Pepper*, the first so-called concept album, and full of drug references. Jagger became increasingly determined to beat them at their own game. Yet it was never really the Stones' own scene.

None of the numbers for the album was written before the group started recording; all they had were a few riffs. Brian was apparently opposed to the whole concept of the album. It was originally intended to be called *Her Satanic Majesty's Request*, but Decca insisted on *Their Satanic Majesties Request* to avoid trouble. The actual album cover was the epitome of sixties pop art and surreal imagery. It featured the Stones in exotic costumes in a dream landscape of flowers and mountains, planets and a rainbow castle. The artwork alone cost £10,000. The original album title was to have been *Cosmic Christmas*.

Side One opened with the long track 'Sing This All Together', originally running to fifteen minutes but now divided in two. It ran without a break into 'Citadel', with its strange rhythm and electronic sound. Bill Wyman's 'In Another Land' was sung by Wyman himself, who explained that it was the interpretation of a man's dream. '2000 Man', about a citizen in AD 2000, had a bright quality, and was followed by the second section of 'Sing This All Together', with its vaguely Eastern sound.

Side Two opens with 'She's A Rainbow', with prominent

piano, 'The Lantern' with its tolling bell at the beginning, and 'Gomper' with its distinctly Indian-influenced sounds. After the exotic '2000 Light Years From Home' came the finale, 'On With The Show'. It was the first album arranged and produced by the Rolling Stones themselves. The complexity of the arrangements is indicated by the fact that the Stones have never performed any of the numbers from *Satanic Majesties* live on stage.

It was during the recording of this album that the Stones had their final showdown with Andrew Oldham, with whom relations had been worsening for some time. He finally walked out, thus severing his links for all practical purposes.

For many fans the album simply didn't work. The Stones' natural idiom was raunchy, sexy rock, strong, immediate beat, direct emotion – not this heady, selfconscious artsy concoction. Bill Wyman later admitted that the Stones were at this time really directionless in musical terms. *Satanic Majesties* was just too far removed from their bluesy rock, and they soon recognized their blunder.

In September the Stones announced their break with Andrew Oldham; they intended to produce all their own records from now on. But in March 1968 the American producer Jimmy Miller was called in.

Only two days after the hearing of his court appeal, Brian Jones collapsed and was rushed to hospital. He had once more overdone things, and seemed to be set upon self-destruction.

The remainder of the band were adjusting to their new-found wealth in more positive ways. Keith was settled into his country house at Redlands, Mick Jagger and Marianne Faithfull in their new Georgian house in Cheyne Walk, Chelsea – and the Elizabethan manor house, Stargrove, near Newbury in Berkshire; Charlie Watts in his country house, once the home of Lord Shawcross.

But 1967 was a year best forgotten.

6

Performance

Following all the publicity, the Stones now went into something of a retreat. They gave very few public concerts; an exception was a surprise appearance at the *New Musical Express* Poll-Winners' Concert, which was in fact their first public performance in the UK for two years – and a resounding success.

The collaboration with their new independent record producer Jimmy Miller on their next album was also highly successful. In May 1968 the single 'Jumpin' Jack Flash' was released, with its beat and lyrics reminiscent of 'Satisfaction', and it soon climbed to Number One in the charts, despite the long gap since their previous single. Here was the abrasiveness of the vintage Stones' sound, prefiguring the androgynous experimentation of the early seventies.

From the early days the Stones had talked about breaking into film, and there had already been one or two attempts – all abortive – to fulfil this dream. There had been a project to be produced by Lionel Bart, and a film of Anthony Burgess' *A Clockwork Orange*. Now they embarked on two contrasting projects. The first was with the darling of the sixties avant-garde cinema, French director Jean-Luc Godard. The film cuts disconcertingly from a South American revolutionary on the run in London to black militants to a woman revolutionary to the Rolling Stones in rehearsal. It was totally a product of its age: an advanced, 'radical' film. In one interview at least Mick Jagger claimed not to know what it all added up to: 'I mean he's completely freaky. I think the idea for the music is great but I don't think it will be the same when it is finished . . . we find the Rolling Stones freaking out at the recording studio. Godard happened to catch us on two very good nights. One night he got us going over this song called "Sympathy For The Devil" . . . he has the whole thing from beginning to end. That's something I've always wanted to do on film.'

Under its original title *One Plus One* the film was first screened at the 1968 London Film Festival. It provoked an incident when Godard discovered that his producers, Michael Pearson and Iain Quarrier, had substituted a freeze-frame ending with the Rolling Stones playing 'Sympathy For The Devil' over it for his own abrupt black-out and ragged sound fade. Jean-Luc Godard punched Quarrier in the face.

But Quarrier remained anxious to capitalize on the Stones' participation in the film, and after a prolonged struggle managed to get the film's title changed to *Sympathy For The Devil*, and to get more material incorporated showing the Rolling Stones. 'We have to consider ten million teeny-boppers in the United States alone.'

For the other film, *Performance*, Jagger was to play a lead role, that of Turner, a rock star in retirement. The film, codirected by Donald Cammell, a friend of Jagger's, and Nicolas Roeg, was to become notorious for its sexual ambivalence. The plot concerned an apparently very masculine London gangster on the run who finds sanctuary in the house of Turner, the ex-pop star. James Fox played opposite Jagger as the fugitive gangster. Warner Brothers funded the project in a moment of inattention, presumably not realizing the decadent atmosphere it was intended to portray.

The core of the film, which was allowed to evolve as they shot it, was the confrontation between Fox and Jagger. At first they were worlds apart, but the pervasive atmosphere of drugs, sexuality and seclusion gradually merged the two personalities. Jagger wore make-up and flamboyant clothes;

a very androgynous young woman lived with him in the house. Fox, the macho gangster, dyed his hair and altered his appearance to elude his pursuers. There were strong elements of camp and homosexuality, and Fox began to take on some of the camp gestures of Turner while Jagger borrowed some of the gangster's violence.

One critic has suggested that the film is a variant on a religious conversion story, with a depraved man of violence saved by learning how to love. His redemption comes through initiation into an exotic bisexual drug-orientated world. Jagger himself suggests that Turner was a projection of Cammell's fantasy of what Jagger imagined himself to be.

As filming continued pressures built up, with the ending still undecided. James Fox was apparently unhappy about the excesses of decadence, the sexual ambivalence. He was not alone in his anxiety. Warner Brothers were horrified when they saw what had been produced, and promptly shelved the finished film. At one point Jagger and Cammell cabled Warners, after they had seen a drastically cut version of the film: 'You seem to want to emasculate (i) the most savage and (ii) the most affectionate scenes in our movie. If *Performance* does not upset audiences it is nothing.' It was two years before *Performance* was released.

A further abortive film project was attempted later in the same year. Starting out from an extravaganza to be called 'The Maxigasm', to be directed by Carlo Ponti, the Stones ended up spending two days filming a television show called 'The Rolling Stones Rock And Roll Circus', produced by Jimmy Miller and directed by Michael Lindsay-Hogg. Once more there was the merging of two worlds, this time circus and rock. The show coupled clowns and Jethro Tull, fire-eaters and the Who, and featured an amazing megastar band comprising John Lennon, Keith Richard, Eric Clapton and drummer Mitch Mitchell. Marianne Faithfull sang 'Something Better', Lennon's superstar group played 'Yer Blues', Yoko Ono wailed to a classical violinist's accompaniment, the Who performed 'A Quick One While He's Away', and the whole show ended with a set from the Stones, including such classics as 'Jumpin' Jack Flash' and 'Sympathy For The Devil'. But this show, too, was shelved, and unlike *Performance* was never released, for reasons that have never been explained.

The Stones seemed to be unable to avoid trouble. In May Brian Jones was busted again, only a year after his previous offence. There were counter accusations that this time it was a plant; although he was apparently becoming increasingly addicted, he had been careful since his previous arrest not to be found in possession of drugs. By now he was habitually incapacitated and more often than not incapable of taking part in recording sessions. A substitute guitarist had to be brought in. The worse his condition, the more he felt he was being squeezed out of the group. The next album, *Beggar's Banquet* (December 1968) did not in fact contain a note played by Jones.

Most damaging to his self-esteem, Brian's own songs were never used by the group. Bill Wyman suffered the same fate — but had greater resilience. By the end of the year, having laid plans to tour again, Jagger and Richard had decided to tell Jones he couldn't come with them because of the difficulties the authorities would make about his drugs record. They informed him that Mick Taylor was prepared to step into his shoes; he seemed resigned to the fact.

Jones' drugs case came up in September. Although the judge directed the jury that the evidence against Brian was merely circumstantial, they found him guilty. But this time the sentence was lenient — £50 fine and £100 costs. Jones continued to claim that the cannabis had been planted.

Jagger believes there was a real effort to destroy the Stones, to make scapegoats of them. And who better to single out than the weakest member, Brian Jones. Jagger sees it as a systematic campaign of harassment, which gave him personally a totally new view of the role of the police.

At about this time Mick's girlfriend Marianne Faithfull became pregnant. The couple went off to Ireland for peace, since the pregnancy was expected to be difficult. Despite this care, Marianne had a miscarriage. Together with Keith Richard and Anita Pallenberg, Mick and Marianne took off for a holiday in Brazil in December. The lonely Brian went to Sri Lanka, once more finding himself a misfit. He was apparently turned away from several hotels in Kandy as he appeared to be a disreputable hippie.

In July the single 'Street Fighting Man', a reflection of the militancy of these years, was released in the States. This was the summer of student riots in the West, the assassinations of Martin Luther King and Robert Kennedy, the overthrow of General de Gaulle in France, the Democratic Convention riots in Chicago. At the height of the Vietnam protests, of the great London Grosvenor Square demo, the number seemed to provide an anthem of protest. It was consequently banned by many American radio stations. Jagger, with mercenary calculation, commented: 'The last time they banned one of our records in America it sold a million.' In an *IT* interview Jagger spoke of the 'energy' he picked up from the rioting students. But the Stones' politics are not so much socialist as anarchist. They are in a way indifferent to external events but assault every idol of bourgeois society. Jagger denied that the Stones were making a political statement:

In America, the rock and roll bands have gotten very political. They express themselves very directly about the Vietnam War. But when I come home to England everything is completely different, so quiet and peaceful. If one lives in such an atmosphere, one has a great detachment from politics and writes completely differently about them.

The single was a track from the new album *Beggar's Banquet*, which was delayed by a long fight between the

Rolling Stones and their record company, Decca, about the cover artwork. Jagger and Richard had decided that it should feature a lavatory wall scrawled with graffiti, including such squibs as 'God rolls his own'. After a long stalemate the Stones finally backed down, and the album was released with a modified cover in the form of an RSVP invitation card. But this marked the end of any hopes of working happily with Decca again. The album's release was celebrated with a medieval banquet in London, with an orgy of custard-pie throwing as its climax.

The opening track of *Beggar's Banquet*, 'Sympathy For The Devil', was also its longest, at over six minutes. Starting with a calypso bongo beat, it built up to a furious piano and bass backing for the number. The album continued with 'No Expectations', a slow, calm number, and with the witty 'Dear Doctor'. The sensual 'Parachute Woman' is a typical Stones blues, featuring Jagger on harmonica. It is followed by 'Jigsaw Puzzle'.

Side Two opens with 'Street Fighting Man', 'Prodigal Son', 'Stray Cat Blues', a wild number in the 'Satisfaction' genre, and a favourite with boppers. The final 'Salt Of The Earth' is quite definitely in the Dylan style.

An outstanding album, *Beggar's Banquet* marked the true arrival of the rolling Stones as an album group rather than solely makers of amazing hit singles. The album had been written and recorded in an intensive period of eight weeks, and mirrored the period of violence and turmoil that followed swiftly upon the summer of Flower Power. The lyrics of 'Sympathy For The Devil' are among the most provocative Jagger has written or sung; it reflected the struggle of blacks for liberation, and he conceded privately it was about the contrasting figures of Enoch Powell and Michael X. 'Stray Cat Blues' was another groupie song; throughout the album there is evidence of a return to a distinctly blues sound.

The Stones were on their way again musically. They turned their backs on the wayward psychedelia of *Their Satanic*

Majesties in favour of their black American beginnings. Here again was the heavy, driving rock their fans expected, and something totally in tune with the restlessness of the times.

In May 1969 Mick Jagger and Marianne Faithfull were charged with possession of cannabis. Jagger accused one of the policemen involved of demanding a bribe. But he was nevertheless found guilty and fined £200. Marianne was acquitted.

In the spring of 1969 Brian stayed at Keith's house in Sussex, Redlands, while his own new home was being renovated. It was perhaps no coincidence that he had purchased Cotchford Farm, once the property of A.A. Milne, who wrote his children's classics *Winnie The Pooh* and *The House At Pooh Corner* while living there. The house spoke of innocence – perhaps a wilful innocence – totally at odds with the dark world now inhabited by Brian Jones.

From the outset Brian was probably the most vulnerable of the Rolling Stones, both physically and emotionally. He was always insecure about his own ability and about the future of the group. And he always felt he had been responsible for starting the Stones, fuelling his resentment at Jagger's unquestioned leadership later. There was also a continuing smart about Anita Pallenberg's leaving him for Keith Richard.

Mick Jagger recognized Brian's craving for attention. He commented later: 'I never really wanted to be the leader, but somehow I automatically got all the attention . . . Brian cared a lot, but it didn't worry me. That was the thing that messed Brian up – because he was desperate for attention. He wanted to be admired and loved . . .'

Brian eventually moved into Cotchford Farm. But the idyllic surroundings contrasted with his own feelings of paranoia. He was beginning to feel that society itself was conspiring against him. He began to depend on Alexis Korner again, to confide in him his fears and his desire to get back to playing hard, black blues music.

On 9 June 1969 Brian's split with the Rolling Stones was

made public. BRIAN JONES QUITS THE STONES AS GROUP CLASH OVER SONGS shouted the *Daily Sketch*. Brian backed up this story: 'I no longer see eye-to-eye with the others over the discs we are cutting.' Jagger's public comment was, 'Brian wants to play music which is more to his tastes rather than always playing ours. So we have decided that it's best that he is free to follow his own inclination.'

Brian's replacement was announced as Mick Taylor, still only twenty, who had been playing bass guitar with John Mayall's Bluesbreakers. Five years later Taylor commented:

> It was hard taking over from Brian Jones. I was certainly made to feel very much aware of it when I joined the Stones – made to feel very conscious that I was following in somebody else's footsteps. But in a sense when I joined the group it was like joining a completely new band that hadn't done any tours for two or three years. I always thought Brian Jones was a very good musician too. I never actually knew him so it wasn't so much of an emotional trauma for me as it was for everybody else.

On 3 July 1969 Brian Jones died. He went for a midnight swim at Cotchford, and was later discovered lying motionless at the bottom of his swimming pool. His girlfriend Anne Wohlin, a Swedish nurse, dived in, pulled him out, and tried to resuscitate him, but to no avail.

Rumours soon multiplied. Stories were circulating that it was suicide. Keith Richard suggested there had been a party going on, and Brian had not been properly looked after. The official version, the coroner's verdict, was death by misadventure. The autopsy revealed 'severe liver dysfunction due to fatty degeneration and ingestion of alcohol and drugs'. His death was caused by 'immersion in fresh water . . . under the influence of drugs and alcohol'. He was twenty-seven.

The Rolling Stones had previously planned a free concert in Hyde Park, London, for 5 July. They had even talked about inviting Brian back to play with them. The first thought now was to cancel the concert: then the idea was mooted of making it a memorial to Brian.

The day before the concert their new single, a double A-side 'Honky Tonk Woman'/'You Can't Always Get What You Want' was released, their first single for thirteen months. It included Mick Taylor on guitar for the first time with them, and a fine sax riff. 'You Can't Always Get What You Want' also used the American soul singer Doris Troy, Al Kooper (ex-Blood, Sweat and Tears) and the London Bach Choir. In a completely different version, the Stones included the same number as 'Country Honk' on *Let It Bleed*.

There was a huge audience, about 500,000 people, in Hyde Park the hot July Saturday of the concert. Hell's Angels were brought in as stewards, and on this occasion did a good job. After the warm-up groups had finished Jagger came forward dressed in white. He read part of Shelley's *Adonais* as a tribute to Brian:

Peace, Peace! he is not dead, he doth not sleep –
    He hath awakened from the dream of life –
'Tis we, who, lost in stormy visions, keep
    With phantoms an unprofitable strife . . .

As he finished, hundreds of white butterflies were released from boxes on the stage.

Later Mick Jagger commented on Brian's death: 'It was a shock when Brian died. I suppose it was the kind of feeling that if anyone was going to die Brian was going to die. You always had the feeling Brian wouldn't live that long. He just lived his life, very fast. He kind of was like a butterfly . . .'

Keith Richard paid tribute to Brian's musical versatility in his *Rolling Stone* interview of 1971:

He was a cat who could play any instrument. It was like 'there it is, music comes out of it, if I work it for a bit, I can do it'. It's him on marimbas on 'Under My Thumb', and mellotron on quite a few things on *Satanic Majesties*. He was the strings on 'Two Thousand Light Years From Home', Brian on mellotron and brass on 'We Love You', all that Arabic riff.

Mick Jagger tried to sum up Brian's difficulties: 'he was desperate for attention. He wanted to be admired and loved and all that . . . which he was by a lot of people, but it wasn't enough for him.'

Brian Jones was buried at Cheltenham, his home town, on 10 July 1969. He wrote an epitaph for himself: 'Please don't judge me too ,harshly.' The minister at the service was unequivocal: 'Brian was the rebel, he had little patience with authority, convention, tradition.'

Mick Jagger was not at the funeral. He and Marianne Faithfull had already left England for Sydney, Australia, where they were to star in the film *Ned Kelly*, about the notorious Australian outlaw. Marianne's husband John Dunbar had announced he was going to divorce her. Soon after arriving in Australia Marianne, who was to play Kelly's sister, took an overdose and almost died as a result. The actress Diane Craig had to take over in her role. During the filming, Mick Jagger was accidentally wounded in his hand.

Following the Hyde Park concert a second Greatest Hits album was released, *Through The Past, Darkly (Big Hits Vol 2)*, with a tribute to Brian Jones on the back of the cover. In October a special promotional album – in a very limited edition of 200 copies – was released for the use of radio stations. Spanning the Stones' history to date, it provided radio producers with examples of their development as a group.

7

Hell's Angels

By the summer of 1969 it was becoming clear that something
had to be done. Nothing seemed to have gone as planned for
the past eighteen months. *Their Satanic Majesties* was more
or less universally panned. *Performance* had been shelved.
Ned Kelly was dismissed. Brian had gone. They had been
busted. Tours seemed to have gone by the board. The only
unqualified success was the new single, 'Honky Tonk
Woman'.

To attempt to put things right again a US tour was put in
motion – the first in two and a half years. The Rolling Stones
were also trying to get shot of Allen Klein as their financial
manager. His nephew, Ronnie Schneider, was hired to produce this new tour. Everything started well. Jagger had his
new, strident songs, never before performed live in the States.
They started at Fort Collins, Colorado, and each gig seemed
to go better than the last. Jagger appeared to become more
and more histrionic in his act, with his studded belt slamming
onto the stage in 'Midnight Rambler' and his heady act as
Lucifer in 'Sympathy For The Devil'. But there were voices of
protest – about the atmosphere of dread and darkness, about
the excessively high ticket prices, and about Jagger's voyage
away from reality.

The climax to the tour came at Madison Square Garden,
New York, on 27 November 1969. Once more the elite of
New York was there to celebrate – Andy Warhol, Leonard
Cohen, Jimi Hendrix, Janis Joplin. Jagger's act was at its

stagiest. He started with his new signature number 'Jumpin' Jack Flash', performed in an outrageous imitation of Dylan's howl. Then came an overtly sexual performance of 'Live With Me', mike squeezed between his legs. Jagger built up to a climax with his violent performance of 'Midnight Rambler', complete with studded belt, a paean of sadism and rape. Then the horrifying 'Sympathy For The Devil'.

Once more the Rolling Stones seemed secure holders of the title 'The World's Greatest Rock Band'. The Beatles were not to tour again. Dylan's future was in doubt. But here were the Stones in all their ferocious power.

It was Jerry Garcia of the Grateful Dead who suggested that the Stones end their US tour with a free concert in San Francisco. Jagger agreed immediately; it would be a fitting climax for the tour. The concert was fixed for 6 December 1969, and the Hell's Angels were asked to look after security.

This was the Stones' answer to Woodstock, and it would also provide a useful finish to the film of the American tour being shot by the Maysles brothers. (The film was later released as *Gimme Shelter*.)

The concert was originally planned for the Golden Gate Park in San Francisco, but the city authorities refused to make the park available to the Rolling Stones. After insurmountable difficulties over an alternative site, a stock-car track called Altamont, fifteen miles east of Berkeley, was offered less than twenty-four hours before the concert was due to start. No one stopped to consider the problems that might arise as a result of the lack of preplanning for the concert at this location.

There were many portents of trouble. Promoters who had staged similar events prophesied disaster. Astrological freaks predicted chaos – the stars pointed to violence and turmoil. There were drugs and pushers in plenty from the very start. And the Hell's Angels were to be paid in beer.

Violence marred the concert from its outset. Squabbles and brawls between fans. Brooding violence from the Hell's

Angels. While Santana were playing, the Hell's Angels weighed in mercilessly on anyone who looked as if he might invade the stage. During Jefferson Airplane's set their vocalist Marty Balin was knocked out by a Hell's Angel. While Mick Jagger was making his way from his helicopter someone punched him in the face.

There was a delay before the Stones appeared. They waited for darkness – and, they hoped, calm – to fall. Perhaps the audience would settle down a bit. When they felt the conditions were right, the Rolling Stones finally appeared, with Mick Jagger garbed in a red velvet cape and cap. He launched into 'Jumpin' Jack Flash', but failed to wrest control from the crowd. The beatings went on.

Real trouble erupted with 'Sympathy For The Devil'. Jagger stopped in mid-song. He had seen a gun in the audience. It belonged to a young black, Meredith Hunter, who was at the concert with his white girlfriend. The Hell's Angels now lost all restraint and turned on their quarry with primitive butchery. They knifed and booted Hunter to pulp.

Jagger was badly shaken by the violence, but was unable to see exactly what was going on. The concert continued, ending with the appalling choice of 'Street Fighting Man'.

Altamont almost marked the end of the Stones. West Coast America attacked them for irresponsibility. David Crosby claimed that they were out of touch with the scene, that they were misguided in inviting the Hell's Angels. 'The major mistake was taking what was essentially a party and turning it into an ego game and a star trip . . . I think they're on a grotesque ego trip' – a view echoed by many others.

Following Altamont, the Rolling Stones flew straight back to Britain and gave two concerts in London. A live album of the tour, *Get Your Ya-Yas Out!*, was issued in September 1970, partly to counter a bootleg LP available in the States. It was recorded at Madison Square Garden on 27 and 28 November 1969, and has all the energy of the Stones' live shows.

Reverberations of Altamont continued to sound over a decade later. In March 1983 a former Hell's Angel testified to a US Senate judiciary committee that: 'There is an open contract on this one rock band leader (Mick Jagger). There have been two attempts to kill him. Eventually it will happen.' The Hell's Angels apparently believe Jagger turned against them after the death of Meredith Hunter at Altamont.

In December 1969 *Let It Bleed* was released. It contained several non-Jagger/Richard numbers — and a variety of backings from girl singers to the London Bach Choir. Originally titled *Sticky Fingers*, *Let It Bleed* opens with 'Gimme Shelter', a rework of 'Under My Thumb', with Keith Richard and Mary Clayton joining Jagger on vocals. 'Love In Vain' by Woody Payne includes Ry Cooder on mandolin, and 'Country Honk' has Mick Taylor on guitar, Byron Berline on fiddle and Nanette Newman and Keith Richard on vocals with Mick. For 'Live With Me' Richard substitutes for Bill Wyman on bass, and Bobby Keys has a fine tenor sax break. 'Let It Bleed' is the only track with Ian Stewart on piano.

Side Two starts with 'Midnight Rambler', played in vintage Stones' style. For 'You Got The Silver' Nicky Hopkins plays piano and organ, and Brian can be heard on autoharp. The number also marked Keith's real debut as solo vocalist. The song was used on the soundtrack of the film *Zabriskie Point*. The Hawaiian sounds of 'Monkey Man' are followed by 'You Can't Always Get What You Want'.

This album only confirmed the reputation of the Stones as the Lords of Misrule. In 'Midnight Rambler' Jagger uses some of the actual words of the original Boston Strangler when he confessed one of his most vicious crimes.

The Stones now also put their new business arrangements in hand. The new company, Rolling Stones Records, was set up. It was announced that Allen Klein and his ABKCO Industries company had no authority to negotiate recording contracts for the Rolling Stones. Plans were made to move to France to avoid the massive tax bills incurred in Britain. And after the years of turbulence, Marianne Faithfull and Mick Jagger finally broke up in 1970.

Possibly Jagger learned something important from the Altamont débâcle. He mellowed. He never again approached the extremes in performance of the 1969 US tour. The 1970s image was more that of the trendy jet-setting superstar than the rebellious troublemaker. He claims not to understand the connections between music and violence. 'I just know that I get very aroused by music, but it doesn't arouse me violently. I never went to a rock 'n' roll show and wanted to smash the windows or beat up anybody afterwards. I feel more sexual than actually physically violent.'

The writer Robert Greenfield gives a snapshot image of the Rolling Stones at this point in their career:

> The Stones, still together today, are separately becoming the people they want to be. Charlie . . . could be drumming with a jazz quartet . . . Bill wears fine clothes, likes white wine, smokes small cigars. Mick Taylor is younger than anyone, as much a part of things as he wants to be, a fine blues guitarist. Keith drives the band on stage, pushes the changes . . . Mick Jagger . . . very much the man of the world, always wherever he wants to be on a given night, in the process of becoming European.

Despite this peaceful image, trouble continued to pursue the Stones. In August 1970 they made a six-week tour of Europe. There was violence in Hamburg, ten arrests in Berlin, injuries in Paris and tear-gas in Milan.

During the year the four films featuring Jagger and the Stones were finally released. *Sympathy For The Devil*, Godard's feature, is not essentially a Stones' film. A critic attempted to explain Godard's purpose in it: 'One is left with the feeling that the film as a whole doesn't add up . . . it is not meant to add up, and it won't . . . we are meant to take the film as it stands, a series of fragmentary fragments [*sic*], and it

81

is for us to edit the film in our own minds.' Film critics apart, *Sympathy For The Devil* is the best record on film of the Rolling Stones at a studio session. Their approach and commitment are there for all to see. It is also the last film record of Brian playing with the Stones.

Performance got a better reception, but was given only limited release in Britain. The critic Alexander Walker attacked it as the 'outcome of an over-developed visual sense and an under-developed moral one', and the *New Yorker* dismissed it as 'one of the more striking pieces of film dopiness and irresponsibility in years', but another critic saw the film as 'the most provocative, searing, uncompromising imaginative vision of the future'.

For *Ned Kelly* Jagger was pilloried. Critics attacked his weedy, non-macho image. Jagger was accused of delivering his lines with 'an almost catatonic lack of expression' (not wholly surprising in the context of Brian Jones' death and Marianne Faithfull's overdose). This was Jagger's first attempt at straight acting, and he and director Tony Richardson were both reckoned to have failed dismally. Jagger was apparently hurt by the critical grilling, which may explain his failure to repeat these experiments with film.

Gimme Shelter, originally intended as a celebration of the Rolling Stones on tour, ended as a grim reminder of the horrors of Altamont. Although it includes the ecstasy of Madison Square Garden, it is finally a dark record. One critic cried in despair, 'I can't write about it any more'. Despite their megastar status, the Stones have still not returned to film-making.

8

It's Only Rock 'n' Roll

Mick Jagger met Bianca Perez Moreno de Macias in Paris in 1970. She came from Nicaragua, studied for a time at the Sorbonne, and then worked in Paris. She was an ex-girlfriend of Michael Caine. By the end of the year there were persistent rumours that Mick and Bianca were going to get married.

Towards the end of 1970 Marsha Hunt, who shot to fame in the rock musical *Hair*, gave birth to a daughter whose father she claimed was Mick Jagger. In July 1973 she took legal steps to establish his paternity. Jagger took counter-measures; the action was finally settled out of court in 1975.

Meanwhile plans were finalized for the Rolling Stones to emigrate to France. They made a farewell tour of England in March 1971, their first in five years. Their own record label, Rolling Stones Records, was now ready for launching. It was to be administered by Marshall Chess of Chess Studios, Chicago. The Stones had cut their ties with their previous record companies, and signed up with the Kinney Group, comprising Warner Brothers, Reprise, Elektra and Atlantic labels. The Stones had also finally dumped Andrew Oldham, and Jimmy Miller was their producer from this point onwards. The new arrangements also made way for the possibility of individual members of the group making solo LPs. In August 1971 *Howlin' Wolf* was released on the Rolling Stones label, with backing supplied by, among others, Charlie Watts and Bill Wyman. The Stones were determined to control their own musical output and also to ensure they saw something more of the financial rewards.

The new label was celebrated with a new maxi single comprising 'Brown Sugar', 'Bitch' and 'Let It Rock', together with the album *Sticky Fingers*. 'Brown Sugar' was attacked by many as both racist and sexist; it is, more accurately, a piece of erotic fantasy featuring whips and cunnilingus. *Sticky Fingers*, released on St George's Day 1971, featured another notorious cover: Andy Warhol artwork of the crutch of a male's pair of jeans, leaving little to the imagination to complete the erotic picture. (The Spanish distributor substituted less offensive artwork, and dropped the track 'Sister Morphine'.) Much of the album had been recorded late in 1969, and it is replete with drug references. But it also showed the Stones on form as an energetic rock band. 'You Can't Hear Me Knocking' had them playing full-out; 'Dead Flowers' and 'Wild Horses' have them playing a kind of country rock.

On the same day that the new company released *Sticky Fingers*, Decca released a new Stones album *Stone Age*, which the Stones vehemently disowned in a special announcement in the music press: 'We didn't know this record was going to be released. It is, in our opinion, below the standard we try to keep up, both in choice of content and cover design.' It added insult to injury by resorting to the graffiti idea for the cover artwork.

After another celebrity party the group finally moved off to France, renting villas in the south. They were determined to escape punitive British taxes, as well as the constant threat of harassment for drug offences by the British police. In 1974 Bill Wyman complained about the financial position they had been in:

After eight years working with one of the world's top bands you would have thought I was set up for life, but I finished up almost broke. We must have sold over

100,000,000 records, but I have never seen 1,000,000 dollars. I had just a couple of grand in the bank, a car, and two houses, but I owed the Inland Revenue a fortune.'

Jagger was meanwhile making plans for his wedding. This time the British press made the Stones appear to be 'deserting' their mother country. Unrealistically, Jagger asked to be allowed a private, secret wedding – while simultaneously ensuring that everyone knew it was about to take place. He took a four-week crash course in Roman Catholicism, and arranged for a planeload of guests to fly to St Tropez for the ceremony.

Once more chaos was the order of the day. Two ceremonies were necessary, both to be held on 12 May. The little council chamber where the mayor of St Tropez was to conduct the civil ceremony was small, and crowded with the world's press and ardent fans long before Mick Jagger and his bride got near it. Jagger's aides attempted to persuade the French authorities to clear the crowded room; but they were given no assistance. The French explained that as it was a public act, the public was entitled to attend. Mick Jagger almost cancelled the proceedings when he saw the chaos, but finally went through with it, to the accompaniment of brawling press photographers and short-tempered reporters.

To avoid similar scenes at his church, the priest locked all the guests into the building, and Jagger had to thump on the door to gain an entrance. The guests at the ensuing party included a cross-section of the contemporary jet set; Ringo Starr, Paul McCartney and Lord Lichfield were among them.

For many at the time, the wedding itself and its jet set trappings symbolized the Stones' new respectability. The rebels had given in. The perpetual adolescents were growing up. Richard Neville (who himself later capitulated to capitalist society) lambasted them in *Oz*, with an angry article titled ON THE DAY THE STONES STOPPED ROLLING. 'The wedding was stark public confirmation of the growing suspicion that Mick Jagger has firmly repudiated the possibilities of a counterculture of which his music is a part.'

On 21 October Bianca Jagger gave birth to a daughter, who was named Jade.

In the summer of 1972 another huge American tour was set in motion. For this tour the band was joined by Bobby Keys, Nicky Hopkins and the American musician, Billy Preston, who started out as a church performer and once worked with such artists as Mahalia Jackson and James Cleveland. The Beatles had brought him in for their sessions for *Let It Be*, and he later recorded more albums for their Apple label.

For the 1972 tour security was taken very seriously indeed. Jagger was concerned for his own safety, and the police laid on heavy guards at each venue. Nevertheless the usual violence occurred time after time. At Vancouver fans tried to break into the stadium, and bottles were thrown onto the stage. In Seattle body searches revealed an automatic pistol and scores of knives. There was a riot in San Diego, and in Montreal French separatist extremists were alleged to have firebombed one of the huge equipment lorries. In Chicago the Stones were put up in fitting style by Hugh Hefner at his Playboy Mansion.

The group tried to learn from the mistakes and the chaos of 1969 for this tour. Ticket sales were strictly organized and controlled. The Stones prepared for the tour with rehearsals in Los Angeles, using a huge empty sound stage at Warner Brothers' Burbank studio. Robert Greenfield described the tour with journalistic flair in his book *A Journey Through America*. But the Stones finally tired of the celebrities such as Truman Capote, Terry Southern and Princess Lee Radziwill who joined the touring party. Keith warned: 'There's no way they're going to be in our company ever again.'

It was noticeable that Jagger's act was now somehow less wild, more controlled. He was more cautious, afraid of the levelled gun, the unlooked for violence. He dropped 'Sympathy For The Devil' from his repertoire because of its Altamont associations. He was careful to avoid approaching too close to his audience, to keep himself from physical contact.

Nevertheless, at Madison Square Garden at the end of this tour, after fifty-one performances in fifty days, Truman Capote, who had been covering the tour for *Rolling Stone* magazine, could still say: 'He's one of the most total actors I've ever seen. He has this remarkable ability to be absolutely totally extroverted.'

The tour became known as the Stones Touring Party, and its tight itinerary was only possible through the use of a chartered jet plane sporting the Stones' new symbol, the now famous lasciviously wicked tongue that Andy Warhol designed for them.

However, when they arrived back in France trouble was awaiting the group. Their efforts to escape the attentions of the drug enforcement agencies were fruitless. The French were now investigating their involvement with drugs, though eventually no actual charges were made against them. But this threat was enough to make the Stones decide that their plans to live part of the year in France should be set aside. They would return home to England. Mick Jagger sounded like a typical tourist returning from the Costa del Sol: 'I don't like the people or the weather in France, and the food's greasy . . .'

In January 1972 they issued the disastrous album *Jamming With Edward*, complete with an excusing letter from Mick Jagger on the cover. The group consisted of Nicky Hopkins, Ry Cooder, Mick Jagger, Bill Wyman and Charlie Watts. Keith Richard failed to turn up for the sessions, and the album needed more than a note from Jagger to excuse it. This travesty was followed the next month by *Milestones*, another appalling Decca compilation. Rolling Stones Records followed up with the single 'Tumbling Dice', backed by 'Sweet

Black Angel', in April. It was their first single for a year.

In May 1972 the Rolling Stones finally resolved their outstanding differences with Allen Klein's ABKCO Industries. *Exile On Main Street* was released a few days later. Mary Whitehouse, at the peak of her populist campaign to clean up British television, protested over alleged obscenities in two tracks on the album. Lord Hill at the BBC suggested that perhaps she heard what she wanted to hear.

The album seems to sum up the group's first ten years, and was cooked up while they were still in their temporary and self-imposed exile in France. Many felt it was simply their best album; its power surprised many listeners accustomed to more tame material. Starting with 'Rocks Off', 'Rip This Joint' follows, with its sheer uninhibited barbarity. 'Rocks Off' is, paradoxically, not about sexual achievement but about impotence. The Stones took the space on this album to look at the other side of sexual boasting and satanic posturing.

In August, Decca issued *Gimme Shelter*, an album trading on the film of the same name but featuring none of the film's actual soundtrack. They followed with yet another bizarre compilation album in October, *Rock 'n' Rolling Stones*.

On 23 December 1972 a disastrous earthquake hit Managua, Nicaragua. Bianca Jagger was appalled by the possibility that members of her family might have been killed in the catastrophe. Mick and Bianca flew to Nicaragua on Boxing Day, but happily discovered that Bianca's mother and other relatives were safe. Moved by the disaster, Jagger organized a benefit concert for its victims, held at the Forum, Los Angeles, and succeeded in raising a total of more than £200,000.

Early in 1973 the Rolling Stones were due to play a major tour of Australia. This seemed very much in question when a ban was suddenly imposed on their entering the country. The ban was lifted equally suddenly and the tour proceeded, with serious rioting at the Adelaide gig. But they were not allowed into Japan because of their drugs record, and a planned tour there had to be cancelled.

In June Keith Richard and Anita Pallenberg were charged with possessing cannabis, heroin and pills, as well as unauthorized firearms. Keith pleaded guilty, and was fined after a court hearing. In July Keith's house Redlands was seriously damaged in a fire. Nobody was hurt, and most of the valuable antique furniture and electrical equipment was salvaged from the blaze. He reacted with scarcely concealed paranoia: 'You've just got this vague feeling that there is somebody trying to get at you. I just try and push it away because there's nothing you can do about it.'

As these events suggested, the Stones were far from finished as a storm centre. In August 1973 came their album *Goat's Head Soup*. The controversial track 'Star, Star' was alleged to allude to groupies' goings on, and was the pretext for its being banned by many radio stations, including BBC Radio 1 and 2. This publicity, as ever, did nothing to hinder the success of their tour, which opened the day after the album was released.

The single 'Angie' was also released in August, and became more of a gossip topic than a musical hit. Everyone wanted to know if it referred to Angela Bowie. The publicity tended to overshadow the release of *Goat's Head Soup* less than a fortnight later.

'Star, Star' had originally been called 'Starfucker'; Atlantic Records not surprisingly objected. Although Mick Jagger at first rejected their arguments, he finally agreed to the new name and overdubbed the unacceptable words on the track. The first tracks on Side One of the album, 'Dancing With Mr D', 'Doo Doo Doo Doo Doo (Heartbreaker)', '100 Years Ago', and 'Coming Down Again' show the Stones experimenting once more with new styles.

Decca again responded with a release of their own, *No Stone Unturned*, an album of B-sides, issued in October 1973.

The Rolling Stones 1973 tour was the most extensive since

1967, and the first tour of the UK since 1971. The band gathered additional musicians: Billy Preston on keyboards, and Bobby Keys, Jim Price and Trevor Lawrence. Their performance at Wembley Stadium in September was particularly impressive.

The Stones had certainly entered a new phase. With the heightened drama of the late sixties dissolved, they seemed to have become simply the world's greatest rock band; no satanic evil, no extraordinary vibrations. Still centre-stage, rumours still focused on them: Mick's marriage was a constant subject for gossip; Mick Taylor was always predicted to be retiring; Ron Wood was said to be planning to join them.

Members of the band were beginning to work on individual albums, a possibility opened up by the creation of Rolling Stones Records. Bill Wyman pulled in Dr John and Leon Rossell to help him; Keith Richard joined Ron Wood on his solo album, *I've Got My Own Album To Do*; Mick featured on a Billy Preston disc and on Keith Moon's album *Like A Rat Up A Pipe*. Bill had issued two singles by 1975, 'White Lightning' and 'Monkey Grip Glue', as well as his album *Monkey Grip*.

In October 1974 the Rolling Stones' new album, *It's Only Rock 'n' Roll*, appeared, the title track having been issued as a single in July. Many fans wrote it off as a total letdown. The title track seems to be a selfconscious attempt to return to early glories, as Mick Taylor surmised. Keith Richard commented perceptively: 'People have such preconceived ideas about what they want from the Rolling Stones that on first hearing our albums don't always come up to these expectations.' The band was rejecting the public pressure to be outrageous *every* time. Now they wanted to simply make enjoyable music – not statements. They started to experiment with new forms and styles – reggae, black street funk.

In December Mick Taylor finally announced he was leaving the Stones. Younger, quiet and reserved, Taylor had joined Wyman and Watts as the background musical force of the Stones behind the more flamboyant Jagger and Richard. When it was suggested that Taylor was dissatisfied with the Stones, Mick Jagger countered by demanding why anyone would willingly leave the Rolling Stones. 'I mean it's not the bloody *army*; it's just a sort of rock 'n' roll band.' In fact Mick Taylor seems to have felt he was underemployed and now wanted to make his own way. But Ron Wood continued to deny stories that he had been asked to take Taylor's place, as did Mick Ronson and Harvey Mandel.

In 1975 the Rolling Stones made their first US tour since their successful Touring Party of 1972. A compilation disc, *Made In The Shade*, preceded them, in an attempt to prepare the way. The 'Tour of the Americas 75' lasted fully three months. Ron Wood joined the band for the tour along with Billy Preston, and Ollie Brown on percussion. Ron fitted in well, with his stage acting and his penchant for riff-playing. Somehow he was a powerful catalyst for Keith.

The Stones once more toured with massive truckloads of staging, lights and sound equipment. The effects had become part of their travelling roadshow. A special stage for their New York and Los Angeles concerts weighed twenty-five tons and itself required three trucks to haul it. For the smaller venues, staging weighed ten tons and measured seventy-one feet in diameter, and was carried in three additional trucks. Sound equipment totalled thirty-two separate cabinets, and weighed eight tons all told. The entire tour was described in superlatives. Audiences aggregated 2,000,000, ticket sales 50,000,000 dollars.

By the end of the year the question of Ron Wood's status had, at least to the public at large, become very muddled. Amid rumours that the Stones were planning a retirement concert, Rod Stewart said he was leaving the Faces because he thought Ron was playing with the Stones again in the new year. But in fact Wood's guest appearances on the 1975 tour were exactly that.

In May 1975 Decca released a single of Stevie Wonder's 'I

Don't Know Why' backed by 'Try A Little Harder'. In June they followed this up with another album, *Metamorphosis*, which consists largely of material never intended for public release. Decca seemingly scooped the bottom of the barrel for out-takes, mistakes and demo recordings. The Stones themselves were overruled by Allen Klein in the selection of tracks for the album.

Decca next released the single 'Out Of Time', and in November another album, *Rolled Gold (The Very Best Of The Rolling Stones)*. This attempted to live up to its pretentious title, and was selected by Alan Fitter and Roy Carr.

Even its title reflects that *Black And Blue* (released 10 April 1976) was a consciously black-influenced album, re-emphasizing the band's beginnings and roots. Once more the cover sparked controversy; in an increasingly feminist decade, a woman photographed in bondage was guaranteed to outrage. The album succeeds best, as ever, when the Stones return to their own musical spirit, when they remould songs to their own purposes rather than merely copy contemporary sounds. One of the album's most successful tracks is 'Melody', with Jagger and Billy Preston crooning together. The single 'Fool To Cry', backed by 'Crazy Mama', was released on the same date as the album.

Lester Bangs wrote perceptively of *Black And Blue*:

> They are still perfectly in tune with the times (ahead sometimes, trendies) and . . . because it's all over, they really don't matter any more or stand for anything, which is certainly lucky for both them and us. I mean, it was a heavy weight to carry for all concerned. This is the first meaningless Stones album.

The Stones were stung into action particularly by the eruption of Punk in the mid 1970s in Britain. Keith claims their response was: 'You want to hear some stripped down rock 'n' roll? Right, we'll give it to you.' The Stones tended to

92

revert to their earlier recording sounds, with a rawer tone in place of the sophisticated and elaborate recordings they had begun to make.

In 1977 the band tried to return to playing smaller venues again. But the worst thing happened: while they were playing in Canada Keith Richard was arrested and charged with possession of heroin. The offence carried a maximum penalty of life imprisonment, and once more the group's future seemed in question. Keith only escaped by agreeing to do a free concert on behalf of the blind, and continuing his treatment for heroin addiction. The treatment apparently succeeded; he had by now been an addict for ten years. He explained its seductive lure in an interview: 'It's passed on from one generation of musicians to the next, because of the ups and downs, the adrenalin, the need to make the gig the next day when you're totally drained.' In fact it was his desire to keep off heroin that was largely responsible for getting the Stones back on the road again in 1981/2. He explained that the logistical difficultties of scoring heroin on the road are enough in themselves to stop him, and anyway the charge from performing is as potent as any drug.

The album *Some Girls*, released in 1978, found the band apparently discovering fresh inspiration in some of their basic sources: the blues, motown, country, Chuck Berry. And it's no accident that the revival centres on an album about 'some girls'. Perhaps Mick's putdowns of women in some of the lyrics of the sixties had been refined and focused. Here are powerful lyrics such as 'Respectable', 'Lies' and the title track 'Some Girls'. 'Respectable' started out as a song taking off from the respectability the Stones are now frequently accused of flaunting. The album also contains the Stones' first outspokenly gay song, 'When The Whip Comes Down'. But overall, the sounds of this album are those of a lean, hard rock band, close to the sound of the Stones in the mid sixties – but far from being merely nostalgic.

In 1979, at the age of twenty-eight, Bianca took out

divorce proceedings against Jagger. She hired a top American divorce lawyer, Marvin Mitchelson, and claimed divorce on the grounds of irreconcilable differences. Mick Jagger had been living with the Texan singer Jerry Hall for two years. Eventually Bianca settled for a payment of £800,000. By 1982 Jagger had a flat in New York where his daughter Jade lived, and a house in the Loire region of France.

Meanwhile, in the same year as Jagger's marriage broke up Keith finally separated from Anita Pallenberg. Anita had now borne him three children: Marlon in 1969, Dandy in 1972 and Tara, who died at the age of three weeks, in 1976. There was a scandal at the end; Anita's seventeen-year-old lover shot himself in her bed in her New York apartment.

Although on leaving the Rolling Stones in 1979 Mick Taylor had promised that his departure had nothing to do with credits and royalties, in 1981 he launched a lawsuit against the group, claiming lost credits and royalties!

New albums continued to appear annually. The 1980 album, *Emotional Rescue*, made little impact. *Tattoo You*, released in September 1981, caused more of a splash. *New Musical Express* commented favourably: 'A good minor Rolling Stones album' and, more significantly, 'There'll never be a major one again'. *Melody Maker* was equally straight-forward: 'The cracks are showing, and they widen with age, but the snarl is still there even if the bite has gone.'

Another megatour of the States got under way in 1981. Some of the results were released on the live album *Still Life* in 1982. Now *Melody Maker* spared no sympathy: 'A parody of the powerful rock 'n' roll band they used to be, the Stones strut and posture, come on bloated like the Barnum and Bailey of rock 'n' roll.' Meanwhile Decca continued to release a stream of compilation albums – in the UK, Germany, Australia, Japan and elsewhere.

The American tour was followed by tours of Europe and the UK, culminating in their first major London appearance for fully six years. In Britain at least it was noticeable that it was not solely the sixties generation that was attending; the Stones attracted a new teenage audience. But their notoriety still pursued them. The Stones were banned from Florence, and carefully frisked by security men in Sweden. They were still the bad boys of rock – for all their forty years.

9

The World's Greatest Rock Band

One of the impressive features of the Stones' music is its very diversity. Just to mention 'Satisfaction', 'Sympathy For The Devil', 'Mother's Little Helper' and 'Dandelion' reveals a spectrum ranging from raunchy, bluesy rock through the apocalyptic and sardonic to the romantic.

The Stones have never totally lost touch with their starting point in the blues, and when they have strayed furthest from it they have quickly returned. Jagger and Richard's first A-side number, 'The Last Time' marked their own capture of the rhythm and blues style to mould it to their own ends, as demonstrated in 'Satisfaction', which was predominantly a rock number with rhythm and blues origins. It was no coincidence that with this number, where they first discovered their distinctive voice, the Rolling Stones shot to real prominence.

Jagger and Richard's most vital achievement was to bring together a truly complementary lyric and music which echoed the needs and desires of its young audience. However else they may have compromised, the Stones have never reverted to the romantic love songs of the fifties. Jagger once repeated the warning of white parents: 'That old idea of not letting white children listen to black music is *true*, because if you want white children to remain what they are, they mustn't.'

But the Stones have also been very skilled at using other people's songs – and making them unmistakably their own. Take, for instance, their recreation of Chuck Berry's 'Talking

About You'. The Stones took it at about half the original speed, added a funky R & B sound, and Mick Jagger's voice added an insinuation never present in the original. Even the words were changed. For Chuck Berry's 'Got such skill, such a beautiful build', Jagger substituted 'Lovely skin, well soaked in gin'.

Other early Berry numbers recorded by the Stones included 'Come On', 'Bye, Bye Johnny', 'Around And Around', 'Down The Road Apiece' and 'Route 66'. They recorded many numbers richly redolent of the American Deep South, looking at it with the romantic eyes of outsiders: 'Little Red Rooster', 'Can I Get A Witness' and 'Down Home Girl', for instance.

When fans have bothered to listen to the lyrics they have often found a strongly masculine, if not outright chauvinist, even sadistic, streak. Besides the advocacy of promiscuity in 'Satisfaction', there is the macho tone of 'Brown Sugar', the unmissable male supremacy in 'Under My Thumb', the sadistic rapist of 'Midnight Rambler', the notorious groupie song 'Star, Star'.

'Street Fighting Man' may have been hailed as a political protest anthem, but that is to ignore the copout line, 'What can a poor boy do except to sing for a rock 'n' roll band?'

Jagger defends his occasional mumbling of the lyrics. He basically doesn't rate them as terribly important, and mumbles when a bad line comes up. He claims to be influenced by an article of Fats Domino: 'You should never sing the lyrics out very clearly.' Jagger is always very anxious not to have to interpret his own lyrics, and he has chosen not to be clear in his delivery: 'I don't really want to say what everything is about.'

It is always Jagger himself who is at the centre of the Stones' live performances. Terry Southern has credited him with 'perhaps the greatest single talent for "putting a song across" of anyone in the history of performing'. Keith Richard recognizes this talent: 'Mick did his thing and I tried to keep the band together. That's always what it's been, basically. If I'm leaping about, it's only because something's going drastically wrong or it's going drastically right.'

Much of Jagger's stage act is purely his own. But he has always admired the performances of such singers as Bo Diddley, Chuck Berry, Little Richard and James Brown. Jagger also recognizes his own remarkable talent: 'Of course I do occasionally arouse primeval instincts . . . most men can do that. They can't do it to so many. I just happen to be able to do it to several thousand people.' He also commented: 'The Rolling Stones on stage isn't the Boston Pops Symphony Orchestra. It's a load of noise. On record it can be quite musical but when you get on stage it's no virtuoso performance. It's a rock and roll act, a very good one and nothing more.' He added ruefully: 'People expect a lot more of us than they do anybody else.'

But Jagger the performer continues unabated. He still has the unmistakable energy and power of his greatest performances. He can still tease and titillate, mock and prance, posture and proclaim. Such a performer hungers for live public appearances.

His stage act is unmistakable. Where does it derive from? Keith Richard denies that it has been consciously developed. Some critics have suggested that it originates in Mick's natural gift for mimicry, a gift his mother noticed at an early age. He can impersonate the great soul singers with extraordinary accuracy – Otis Redding, Solomon Burke and Marvin Gaye, for example. He was greatly impressed the first time he saw James Brown in action, and adapted his own act in response. He has said in an interview that when he is playing he reverts to feeling like a ten-year-old boy.

But Robert Christgau has suggested a flaw within Jagger's music:

All of them . . . were attracted to the gruff, eloquent directness of so much black music . . . The aggressiveness and sexuality of the form were [Jagger's] but the sincerity was beyond him – partly because he was white and English, and especially because he was Mick Jagger. He loved black music for its sincerity, yet its sincerity was the ultimate object of his pervasive anger. He wanted what he couldn't have and felt detached even from his own desire.

Of equal importance to the Rolling Stones' sound has been Keith Richard. Though he has never claimed the public spotlight in the same way as Jagger, it has been his musicianship that has steered the Stones throughout their unprecedented career. Often, within the songwriting partnership, it was the music that came first, with Keith providing the music, the mood and perhaps a key phrase, to which Jagger added the lyrics. Keith is also a masterly guitarist, and the musical director at rehearsals. Ian Stewart commented in a *Sunday Times* interview: 'Keith is just the ultimate rhythm guitar player. He concentrates on laying it down. On a good night, if he lays down something well it's laid down the way nobody else can do it.'

Stewart went on to suggest that 'if Brian Jones, Bill Wyman, Charlie Watts and myself had never existed on the face of this earth, Mick and Keith would still have had a group that looked and sounded exactly like the Rolling Stones'. Certainly Keith and Mick have a closeness which must not be ignored. When they are credited as producers of a record, they dub themselves 'The Glimmer Twins'.

Of Charlie Watts, Robert Greenfield says: 'Watts is still very much the person he was before it all began, and yet very changed by the years of touring, recording and notoriety . . . Protected for a decade in order to concentrate on playing the drums, he possesses a childlike innocence that is beautiful.'

In the late sixties and early seventies, when political stances were *de rigeur*, when Vietnam was the slogan, when Nixon was the villain, the Stones were frequently catechized about their political stance. Keith Richard expressed their attitude towards their lyrics and their commitment: 'The music says something very basic and simple . . . It's all there, you've only got to look at what's in front of you. And that's all we've ever been trying to do. Not trying to tell people where to go or which way to go, because I don't know. We're all following . . .'

And the satanic reputation? Keith again: 'Before, when we were just innocent kids, they're saying, "They're evil, they're evil". Oh, I'm evil, really? So that makes you start thinking about evil.'

Paul Williams commented: 'The Rolling Stones, during their fat years, constantly gave and then reinforced the impression that they were going through the exact same life experiences as me and coming to the same conclusions – and that at the same time they were also infinitely-more-than-me, all-wise, all-experiencing, all-encompassing.'

After Altamont the band changed. It came under the influence of different movements in the musical world. It took in reggae, disco, New Wave as each came along. The superbly polished group could now turn out as polished a performance in concert as on disc. Jagger tries to defend the change:

We're not *that* band any more, anyway. We're a bunch of different bands. English reviewers seem to have this weird idea of the Rolling Stones as being this band and we've never been *that* band, but they imagine we are. We can do *that* band if we wanna . . . I don't see why we can't make a record that *doesn't* sound like the Rolling Stones. We're not a *brand,* like HP Sauce or something.

Keith Richard expressed much the same sentiment:

When you've been around as long as we have, people have got their own fixed idea of what they want from the Stones and it's never anything new, even though they do really want it, they still compare it with this big moment in the backseat of a car fifteen years ago and it's never as good as then. There's so much nostalgia connected with it that you can't possibly fight, so you have to sometimes let the record seep into their lives . . .

How have the Rolling Stones earned the right to the title 'The Greatest Rock and Roll Band in the World'? Not merely by their records, TV shows and films. It is their live shows that have consistently marked them out as the most exciting band around. In the seventies, with their emphasis on ever more extravagant tours, they coined the slogan 'It's only rock 'n' roll but it's expensive'. They also claimed a record for being the loudest rock band in the world, with a peak of 120 decibels recorded at Earl's Court, London, in 1976. Their tours now take something like fifty people to get on the road, plus massive logistical backup. It's hardly surprising that, with this size of venture, tours have become steadily less frequent.

And how is it that the Rolling Stones have survived as a group for more than twenty years? Bill Wyman volunteers one possible answer: 'A lot of groups live together practically . . . We just split to various parts of the world when we are not working. Then when we get back together again it's good fun.'

Keith Richard similarly explains: 'One of the reasons we still play together, you know, is that we actually enjoy play-ing together. It's still fun for us, like a very well paid hobby.' He adds, 'We're still trying to make the Stones a better band – you wouldn't get these guys to do it if they thought they'd reached a point of no return.'

How long can the Rolling Stones continue? The question has been posed many times in the last decade. Jagger once threatened he would quit when he reached thirty-three. Later he promised that it wouldn't go on for ever, and objected to being treated like the 'Godfather of Pop'. Keith Richard, in a recent interview, questioned whether being a middle-aged rock 'n' roller is as ridiculous as most people have made it out to be. 'Nobody's ever done it this long before, and no doubt people thought the same about jazz in the twenties, that it was inconceivable that the musicians could keep going. But I played with Muddy Waters in Chicago and he's no young guy any more, but he's playing as good as ever. And if he can do it, I'm sure I can . . .'

Keith has another answer too: 'Once you're in front of an audience, you forget all of it. That's why the Rolling Stones will go on and on. We don't do anything better than playing to people.'

As to being rich and playing rock – a contradiction for many critics – Jagger rejects these as incompatibles: 'First of all, you really don't need a lot of money to make music, and secondly, getting rich, very rich, is an integral part of the original rock 'n' roll dream . . . Now if I did it for the money and nothing else, I wouldn't be playing with the Rolling Stones, I could go out and do say, the Empire Pool, Wembley . . . on my own, charge a dollar a seat and still make money.'

One of the 1982 tour interviews put it very succinctly: Mick is not an artist but a performer. He has to feed on other people's ideas. And he knows that sooner or later he will have to move into another area.

Perhaps the most unglamorous answer is that they will break up when they can afford to – having accustomed themselves to the high life of the jet set.

The Stones may have been knocked by the English critics in their second decade – but the fact remains that they have continued to record, to perform and to sell. Their albums regularly notch up 2,000,000 sales worldwide.

Discography UK

Singles

June 1963
Come On/I Want To Be Loved   Decca F 11675

November 1963
I Wanna Be Your Man/Stoned   Decca F 11764

February 1964
Not Fade Away/Little By Little   Decca F 11845

July 1964
It's All Over Now/Good Times, Bad Times   Decca F 11934

November 1964
Little Red Rooster/Off The Hook   Decca F 12014

February 1965
The Last Time/Play With Fire   Decca F 12104

August 1965
(I Can't Get No) Satisfaction/The Spider And The Fly
Decca F 12220

October 1965
Get Off Of My Cloud/The Singer Not The Song
Decca F 12263

February 1966
19th Nervous Breakdown/As Tears Go By   Decca F 12331

May 1966
Paint It Black/Long, Long While   Decca F 12395

September 1966
Have You Seen Your Mother, Baby?/
Who's Driving Your Plane   Decca F 12497

January 1967
Let's Spend The Night Together/Ruby Tuesday
Decca F 12546

August 1967
We Love You/Dandelion   Decca F 12654

May 1968
Jumpin' Jack Flash/Child Of The Moon   Decca F 12782

July 1969
Honky Tonk Women/
You Can't Always Get What You Want   Decca F 12952

July 1970
Street Fighting Man/Surprise, Surprise   Decca F 13203

April 1973
Sad Day/You Can't Always Get What You Want
Decca F 13404

May 1975
I Don't Know Why/Try A Little Harder   Decca F 13584

September 1975
Out Of Time/Jiving Sister Fanny   Decca F 13597

April 1976
Honky Tonk Women/Sympathy For The Devil
Decca F 13635
Reissue

April 1976
A Quarter To Three/Soul Satisfying   RS 19119
(Bill Wyman solo)

April 1976
Fool To Cry/Crazy Mama   RS 19121

September 1976
Apache Woman/Soul Satisfying   RS 19303
(Bill Wyman solo)

May 1978
Miss You/Girl With The Faraway Eyes   EMI 2808

November 1970
Jagger: Memo from Turner/Natural Magic   Decca F 13067

EPs

January 1964
The Rolling Stones   Decca DFE 8560
Bye Bye Johnny
Money
You Better Move On
Poison Ivy

August 1964
Five by Five   Decca DFE 8590
If You Need Me
Empty Heart
Confessin' The Blues
Around And Around

June 1965
Got Live If You Want It!   Decca DFE 8620
We Want The Stones
Everybody Needs Somebody To Love
Pain In My Heart
Route 66
I'm Moving On
I'm Alright

June 1972
Street Fighting Man   Decca F 13195
Street Fighting Man
Surprise, Surprise

Albums

September 1965

Out Of Our Heads   Decca LK 4733
She Said Yeah
Mercy, Mercy
Hitch Hike
That's How Strong My Love Is
Good Times
Gotta Get Away
Talkin' 'Bout You
Cry To Me
Oh Baby (We Got A Good Thing Going)
Heart Of Stone
The Under Assistant West Coast Promotion Man
I'm Free

April 1966

Aftermath   Decca SKL 4786
Mother's Little Helper
Stupid Girl
Lady Jane
Under My Thumb
Doncha Bother Me
Goin' Home
Flight 505
High And Dry
Out Of Time
It's Not Easy
I Am Waiting
Take It Or Leave It
Think
What To Do

November 1966
Big Hits (High Tide And Green Grass)   Decca TXS 101
Have You Seen Your Mother, Baby?
Paint It Black
It's All Over Now
The Last Time
Heart Of Stone
Not Fade Away
Come On
(I Can't Get No) Satisfaction
Get Off Of My Cloud
As Tears Go By
19th Nervous Breakdown
Lady Jane
Time Is On My Side
Little Red Rooster

January 1967
Between The Buttons   Decca LK 4852
Yesterday's Papers
My Obsession
Back Street Girl
Connection
She Smiled Sweetly
Cool, Calm and Collected
All Sold Out
Please Go Home
Who's Been Sleeping Here?
Complicated
Miss Amanda Jones
Something Happened To Me Yesterday

December 1967
Their Satanic Majesties Request   Decca TXS 103
Sing This All Together
Citadel
In Another Land
2000 Man
Sing This All Together (See What Happens)
She's A Rainbow
The Lantern
Gomper
2000 Light Years From Home
On With The Show

December 1968
Beggars Banquet   Decca SKL 4955
Sympathy For The Devil
No Expectations
Dear Doctor
Parachute Woman
Jigsaw Puzzle
Street Fighting Man
Prodigal Son
Stray Cat Blues
Factory Girl
Salt Of The Earth

September 1969
Through The Past Darkly
(Big Hits Vol. 2)   Decca SKL 5019
Jumpin' Jack Flash
Mother's Little Helper
2000 Light Years From Home
Let's Spend The Night Together
You Better Move On
We Love You
Street Fighting Man
She's A Rainbow
Ruby Tuesday
Dandelion
Sittin' On A Fence
Honky Tonk Women

December 1969
Let It Bleed   Decca SKL 5025
Gimme Shelter
Love in Vain
Country Honk
Live With Me
Let It Bleed
Midnight Rambler
You Got The Silver
Monkey Man
You Can't Always Get What You Want

September 1970
Get Yer Ya-Yas Out!   Decca SKL 5065
Jumpin' Jack Flash
Carol
Stray Cat Blues
Love In Vain
Midnight Rambler
Sympathy For The Devil
Live With Me
Little Queenie
Honky Tonk Women
Street Fighting Man

April 1971
Stone Age   Decca SKL 5084
Look What You've Done
It's All Over Now
Confessin' The Blues
One More Try
As Tears Go By
The Spider And The Fly
My Girl
Paint It Black
If You Need Me
The Last Time
Blue Turns To Grey
Around And Around

October 1972
Gimme Shelter   Decca SKL 5101
Jumpin' Jack Flash
Love In Vain
Honky Tonk Women
Street Fighting Man
Sympathy For The Devil
Gimme Shelter
Under My Thumb
I've Been Loving You Too Long
Fortune Teller
Lady Jane
(I Can't Get No) Satisfaction

February 1972
Milestones   Decca SKL 5098
Satisfaction
She's A Rainbow
Under My Thumb
I Just Want To Make Love To You
Yesterday's Papers
I Wanna Be Your Man
Time Is On My Side
Get Off Of My Cloud
Not Fade Away
Out Of Time
She Said Yeah
Stray Cat Blues

October 1972
Rock 'n' Rolling Stones   Decca SKL 5149
Route 66
The Under Assistant West Coast Promotion Man
Come On
Talkin' 'Bout You
'Bye Bye Johnny
Down The Road
I Just Wanna Make Love To You
Everybody Needs Somebody To Love
Oh Baby (We Got A Good Thing Goin')
19th Nervous Breakdown
Little Queenie
Carol

October 1973
No Stone Unturned   Decca SKL 5173
Poison Ivy
The Singer Not The Song
Surprise, Surprise
Child Of The Moon
Stoned
Sad Day
Money
Congratulations
I'm Movin' On
2120 South Michigan Avenue
Long Long While
Who's Driving Your Plane?

114

July 1975
Metamorphosis   Decca SKL 5212
Out Of Time
Don't Lie To Me
Some Things Just Stick In Your Mind
Each And Every Day Of The Year
Heart Of Stone
I'd Much Rather Be With The Boys
(Walkin' Thru' The) Sleepy City
We're Wastin' Time
Try A Little Harder
I Don't Know Why
If You Let Me
Jiving Sister Fanny
Downtown Suzie
Family
Memo From Turner
I'm Going Down

November 1975
Rolled Gold (The Very Best Of The Rolling Stones)
Decca ROST 1/2
Come On
I Wanna Be Your Man
Not Fade Away
Carol
It's All Over Now
Little Red Rooster
Time Is On My Side
The Last Time
(I Can't Get No) Satisfaction
Get Off Of My Cloud
19th Nervous Breakdown
As Tears Go By
Under My Thumb
Lady Jane
Out Of Time
Paint It Black
Have You Seen Your Mother, Baby?
Let's Spend The Night Together
Ruby Tuesday
Yesterday's Papers
We Love You
She's A Rainbow
Jumpin' Jack Flash
Honky Tonk Women
Sympathy For The Devil
Street Fighting Man
Midnight Rambler
Gimme Shelter

116

1982
Stones Story   Decca 6640 030
Tell Me
Everybody Needs Somebody To Love
Play With Fire
Mother's Little Helper
Heart Of Stone
No Expectations
Surprise, Surprise
High And Dry
Something Happened To Me Yesterday
Sitting On A Fence
2000 Light Years From Home
She Smiled Sweetly
Sing This All Together
Take It Or Leave It
Dandelion
I Just Want To Make Love To You
Off The Hook
Stray Cat Blues
Connection
Cool, Calm and Collected
I am Waiting
Dear Doctor
Flight 505
The Under Assistant West Coast Promotion Man
All Sold Out
You Can't Always Get What You Want

1982

The Rolling Stones In Concert   Decca 6.28565 DT
Under My Thumb
Get Off Of My Cloud
Lady Jane
Not Fade Away
I've Been Loving You Too Long
Fortune Teller
The Last Time
19th Nervous Breakdown
Time Is On My Side
I'm Alright
Have You Seen Your Mother, Baby?
(I Can't Get No) Satisfaction
Jumpin' Jack Flash
Carol
Stray Cat Blues
Love In Vain
Midnight Rambler
Sympathy For The Devil
Live With Me
Little Queenie
Honky Tonk Women
Streetfighting Man

March 1983

The Rolling Stones 1965/70   Philips 6495 098

(I Can't Get No) Satisfaction
Get Off Of My Cloud
As Tears Go By
19th Nervous Breakdown
Out Of Time
Lady Jane
Let's Spend The Night Together
Paint It Black
Ruby Tuesday
Yesterday's Paper
Jumpin' Jack Flash
Sympathy For The Devil
Honky Tonk Women
Gimme Shelter

Released on Rolling Stones Records (UK)

Singles

April 1971
Brown Sugar/Bitch [Let It Rock]   RS 19100

April 1972
Tumbling Dice/Sweet Black Angel   RS 19103

August 1973
Angie/Silver Train   RS 19105

July 1974
It's Only Rock 'n' Roll/Through The Lonely Nights
RS 19114

September 1978
Respectable/When The Whip Comes Down   EMI 2861

November 1979
Run Rudolph Run RSR 102
(Keith Richard solo)

June 1980
Emotional Rescue/Down In The Hole   RSR 105

Albums

April 1971
Sticky Fingers   COC 59100
Brown Sugar
Sway
Wild Horses
Can't You Hear Me Knocking
You Gotta Move
Bitch
I Got The Blues
Sister Morphine
Dead Flowers
Moonlight Mile

May 1972
Exile On Main Street   COC 69100
Rocks Off
Rip This Joint
Shake Your Hips
Casino Boogie
Tumbling Dice
Sweet Virginia
Torn And Frayed
Sweet Black Angel
Loving Cup
Happy
Turd On The Run
Ventilator Blues
I Just Want To See His Face
Let It Loose
All Down The Line
Stop Breaking Down
Shine A Light
Soul Survivor

August 1973
Goat's Head Soup   COC 59101
Dancing with Mr D
100 Years Ago
Coming Down Again
Doo Doo Doo Doo Doo (Heartbreaker)
Angie
Silver Train
Hide Your Love
Winter
Can You Hear The Music
Star, Star

October 1974
It's Only Rock 'n' Roll   COC 59103
If You Can't Rock Me
Ain't Too Proud To Beg
It's Only Rock 'n' Roll
Till The Next Goodbye
Time Waits For No One
Luxury
Dance Little Sister
If You Really Want To Be My Friend
Short and Curlies
Fingerprint File

June 1975
Made In The Shade   COC 59104
Brown Sugar
Tumbling Dice
Happy
Dance Little Sister
Wild Horses
Angie
Bitch
It's Only Rock 'n' Roll
Doo Doo Doo Doo Doo (Heartbreaker)
Rip This Joint

April 1976
Black And Blue   COC 59106
Hot Stuff
Hand Of Fate
Cherry Oh Baby
Memory Motel
Hey Negrita
Melody
Fool To Cry
Crazy Mama

September 1977
Love You Live   COC 89101
Introduction
Honky Tonk Women
If You Can't Rock Me
Get Off Of My Cloud
Happy
Hot Stuff
Star, Star
Tumbling Dice
Fingerprint File
You Gotta Move
You Can't Always Get What You Want
Mannish Boy
Crackin' Up
Little Red Rooster
Around And Around
It's Only Rock 'n' Roll
Brown Sugar
Jumpin' Jack Flash
Sympathy For The Devil

May 1978
Time Waits For No One: Anthology 1971–1977
COC 59107
Time Waits For No One
Bitch
All Down The Line
Dancing With Mr D
Angie
Star, Star
If You Can't Rock Me/Get Off Of My Cloud
Hand Of Fate
Crazy Mama
Fool To Cry

June 1978
Some Girls   CUN 39108
Miss You
When The Whip Comes Down
Imagination
Some Girls
Lies
Far Away Eyes
Respectable
Before They Make Me Run
Beast Of Burden
Shattered

June 1980
Emotional Rescue   CUN 39111
Dance
Summer Romance
Send It To Me
Let Me Go
Indian Girl
Where The Boys Go
Down The Hole
Emotional Rescue
She's So Cold
All About You

September 1981
Tattoo You   CUN 39114
Start Me Up
Hang Fire
Slave
Little T & A
Black Limousine
Neighbours
Worried About You
Tops
Heaven
No Use In Crying
Waiting On A Friend

May 1981
Sucking In The Seventies   CUN 39112
Shattered
Everything Is Turning To Gold
Hot Stuff
Time Waits For No One
Fool To Cry
Mannish Boy
When The Whip Comes Down
If I Was A Dancer (Dance Part 2)
Beast Of Burden

June 1982
Still Life   CUN 39115
Under My Thumb
Let's Spend The Night Together
Shattered
Twenty Flight Rock
Going To A Go Go
Let Me Go
Time Is On My Side
Imagination
Start Me Up
Satisfaction

Other Albums

August 1971
The London Howlin' Wolf Sessions   COC 49101
With Bill Wyman, Charlie Watts and Ian Stewart

January 1972
Jamming With Edward   COC 39100
Featuring Nicky Hopkins, Ry Cooder, Mick Jagger, Bill
Wyman and Charlie Watts

February 1976
Stone Alone   COC 59105
(Bill Wyman solo album)
A Quarter To Three
Gimme Just One Chance
Soul Satisfying
Apache Woman
Every Sixty Seconds
Get It On
Feet
Peanut Butter Time
Wine & Wimmen
If You Wanna Be Happy
What's The Point
No More Foolin'

May 1974
Monkey Grip   COC 59102
(Bill Wyman album)
I Wanna Get Me A Gun
Crazy Woman
Pussy
Mighty Fine Time
Monkey Grip Glue
What A Blow
White Lightnin'
I'll Pull You Thro'
It's A Wonder

Discography USA

Singles

March 1964
Not Fade Away/I Wanna Be Your Man   London 9657

June 1964
Tell Me/I Just Want To Make Love To You   London 9682

July 1964
It's All Over Now/Good Times, Bad Times   London 9687

September 1964
Time Is On My Side/Congratulations   London 9708

December 1964
Heart Of Stone/What A Shame   London 9725

March 1965
The Last Time/Play With Fire   London 9741

May 1965
(I Can't Get No) Satisfaction/
The Under Assistant West Coast Promotion Man
London 9766

September 1965
Get Off Of My Cloud/I'm Free   London 9792

December 1965
As Tears Go By/Gotta Get Away   London 9808

February 1966
19th Nervous Breakdown/Sad Day   London 9823

April 1966
Paint It Black/Stupid Girl   London 901

June 1966
Mother's Little Helper/Lady Jane   London 902

September 1966
Have You Seen Your Mother, Baby, Standing In The
Shadow?/Who's Driving Your Plane?   London 903

January 1967
Let's Spend The Night Together/Ruby Tuesday
London 904

August 1967
We Love You/Dandelion   London 905

November 1967
She's A Rainbow/2000 Light Years From Home
London 906

December 1967
In Another Land/The Lantern   London 907

May 1968
Jumpin' Jack Flash/Child Of The Moon   London 908

August 1968
Street Fighting Man/No Expectations   London 909

July 1969
Honky Tonk Women/
You Can't Always Get What You Want   London 910

May 1971
Brown Sugar/Let It Rock   RL 19100

June 1971
Wild Horses/Sway   RLS 101

April 1972
Tumbling Dice/Sweet Black Angel   RLS 19103

June 1972
Happy/All Down The Line   RLS 19104

August 1973
Angie/Silver Train   RLS 19105

December 1973
Heartbreaker/Dancing With Mr. D   RS 19109

July 1974
It's Only Rock 'n' Roll/Through The Lonely Nights
RS 19301

October 1974
Ain't Too Proud To Beg/Dance Little Sister   RS 19302

November 1974
White Lightnin'/Pussy   RS 19115

May 1975
I Don't Know Why/Try A Little Harder   ABKCO 4701

September 1975
Out Of Time/Jiving Sister Fanny   ABCKO 4702

April 1976
Fool To Cry/Hot Stuff   RS 19304

April 1976
Fool To Cry/Crazy Mama   ST DSKO 31990 PR

April 1976
A Quarter To Three/Soul Satisfying   RS 19119

September 1976
Apache Woman/Soul Satisfying   RS 19303
(Bill Wyman solo)

May 1978
Miss You/Girl With The Faraway Eyes   RS 19306

November 1978
Beast Of Burden/When The Whip Comes Down   RS 19309

Albums

May 1964
The Rolling Stones   London PS 375
Not Fade Away
Route 66
I Just Want To Make Love To You
Honest I Do
Now I've Got A Witness
Little By Little
I'm A King Bee
Carol
Tell Me
Can I Get A Witness
You Can Make It If You Try
Walking The Dog

October 1964
12 × 5   London PS 402
Around And Around
Confessin' The Blues
Empty Heart
Time Is On My Side
Good Times, Bad Times
It's All Over Now
2120 South Michigan Avenue
Under The Boardwalk
Congratulations
Grown Up Wrong
If You Need Me
Susie Q

February 1965
The Rolling Stones, Now!   London PS 420
Everybody Needs Somebody To Love
Down Home Girl
You Can't Catch Me
Heart Of Stone
What A Shame
Mona, I Need You Baby
Down The Road Apiece
Off The Hook
Pain In My Heart
Oh Baby (We Got A Good Thing Goin')
Little Red Rooster
Surprise, Surprise

July 1965
Out Of Our Heads   London PS 429
Mercy Mercy
Hitch Hike
The Last Time
That's How Strong My Love Is
Good Times
I'm All Right
Satisfaction
Cry To Me
The Under Assistant West Coast Promotion Man
Play With Fire
The Spider And The Fly
One More Try

November 1965
December's Children   London PS 451
She Said Yeah
Talkin' 'Bout You
You Better Move On
Look What You've Done
The Singer Not The Song
Route 66
Get Off Of My Cloud
I'm Free
As Tears Go By
Gotta Get Away
Blue Turns To Grey
I'm Moving On

March 1965
Big Hits (High Tide and Green Grass)   London NPS 1
The Last Time
As Tears Go By
Time Is On My Side
It's All Over Now
Tell Me
19th Nervous Breakdown
Heart Of Stone
Get Off Of My Cloud
Not Fade Away
Good Times, Bad Times
Play With Fire

June 1966
Aftermath   London PS 476
Paint It Black
Stupid Girl
Lady Jane
Under My Thumb
Doncha Bother Me
Think
Flight 505
High And Dry
It's Not Easy
I Am Waiting
Going Home

November 1966
Got Live If You Want It!   London PS 493
Under My Thumb
Get Off Of My Cloud
Lady Jane
Not Fade Away
I've Been Loving You Too Long
Fortune Teller
The Last Time
19th Nervous Breakdown
Time Is On My Side
I'm Alright
Have You Seen Your Mother, Baby, Standing In The
    Shadow?
(I Can't Get No) Satisfaction

January 1967
Between The Buttons   London PS 499
Let's Spend The Night Together
Yesterday's Papers
Ruby Tuesday
Connection
She Smiled Sweetly
Cool, Calm and Collected
All Sold Out
My Obsession
Who's Been Sleeping Here?
Complicated
Miss Amanda Jones
Something Happened To Me Yesterday

November 1967
Their Satanic Majesties Request   London NPS 2
Sing This All Together
Citadel
In Another Land
2000 Man
Sing This Altogether (See What Happens)
She's A Rainbow
The Lantern
Gomper
2000 Light Years From Home
On With The Show

June 1967
Flowers   London PS 509
Ruby Tuesday
Have You Seen Your Mother, Baby?
Let's Spend The Night Together
Lady Jane
Out Of Time
My Girl
Back Street Girl
Please Go Home
Mother's Little Helper
Take It Or Leave It
Ride On, Baby
Sittin' On A Fence

November 1968
Beggars Banquet   London PS 539
Sympathy For The Devil
No Expectations
Dear Doctor
Parachute Woman
Jigsaw Puzzle
Street Fighting Man
Prodigal Son
Stray Cat Blues
Factory Girl
Salt Of The Earth

September 1969
Through The Past Darkly (Big Hits Vol. 2)   London NPS 3
Honky Tonk Women
Paint It Black
Street Fighting Man
She's A Rainbow
Jumpin' Jack Flash
Dandelion
Ruby Tuesday
Have You Seen Your Mother, Baby?
Let's Spend The Night Together
2000 Light Years From Home
Mother's Little Helper

November 1969
Let it Bleed   London NPS 4
Gimme Shelter
Love In Vain
Country Honk
Live With Me
Let It Bleed
Midnight Rambler
You Got The Silver
Monkey Man
You Can't Always Get What You Want

September 1970
Get Yer Ya-Yas Out!   London NPS 4
Jumpin' Jack Flash
Carol
Stray Cat Blues
Love In Vain
Midnight Rambler
Sympathy For The Devil
Live With Me
Little Queenie
Honky Tonk Women
Street Fighting Man

June 1971
Sticky Fingers   COC 59100 (Rolling Stones Records)
Brown Sugar
Sway
Wild Horses
Can't You Hear Me Knocking
You Gotta Move
Bitch
I Got The Blues
Sister Morphine
Dead Flowers
Moonlight Mile

January 1972
Jamming With Edward   COC 39100
The Boudoir Stomp
It Hurts Me Too
Edward's Thump It
Blow With Ry
Interlude à la El Hopo
Highland Fling
(Features Nicky Hopkins, Ry Cooder, Mick Jagger, Bill
Wyman, Charlie Watts)

November 1971

The London Howlin' Wolf Sessions   Chess CH 60008
Rockin' Daddy
I Ain't Superstitious
Sittin' On Top Of The World
Worried About My Baby
What A Woman!
Poor Boy
Built For Comfort
Who's Been Talking
The Red Rooster
Do The Do
Highway 49
Wang-Dang-Doodle
(Features Howlin' Wolf, Eric Clapton, Steve Winwood, Bill
Wyman, Charlie Watts, Hubert Sumlin, Jeffrey Carp, Ian
Stewart)

November 1971

Brian Jones Presents the Pipes of Pan in Joujouka
COC 49100
Recordings of the Master Musicians of Joujouka, Morocco

May 1972
Exile On Main Street   COC 2-2900
Rocks Off
Rip This Joint
Shake Your Hips
Casino Boogie
Tumbling Dice
Sweet Virginia
Torn And Frayed
Sweet Black Angel
Loving Cup
Happy
Turd On The Run
Ventilator Blues
I Just Want To See His Face
Let It Loose
All Down The Line
Stop Breaking Down
Shine A Light
Soul Survivor

Hot Rocks 1964–1971   London 2PS 606/7
Time Is On My Side
Heart Of Stone
Play With Fire
(I Can't Get No) Satisfaction
As Tears Go By
Get Off Of My Cloud
Mother's Little Helper
19th Nervous Breakdown
Paint It Black
Under My Thumb
Ruby Tuesday
Let's Spend The Night Together
Jumpin' Jack Flash
Street Fighting Man
Sympathy For The Devil
Gimme Shelter
Midnight Rambler
You Can't Always Get What You Want
Brown Sugar
Wild Horses

December 1972
More Hot Rocks   London 2PS 626/627
Tell Me
Not Fade Away
The Last Time
It's All Over Now
Good Times, Bad Times
I'm Free
Out Of Time
Lady Jane
Sittin' On A Fence
Have You Seen Your Mother, Baby, Standing In The
    Shadow?
Dandelion
We Love You
She's A Rainbow
2000 Light Years From Home
Child Of The Moon
No Expectations
Let It Bleed
What To Do
Money
Come On
Fortune Teller
Poison Ivy
Bye Bye Johnny
I Can't Be Satisfied
Long Long While

August 1973
Goats Head Soup   COC 59101
Dancing With Mr D
100 Years Ago
Coming Down Again
Doo Doo Doo Doo Doo (Heartbreaker)
Angie
Silver Train
Hide Your Love
Winter
Can You Hear The Music
Star, Star

May 1974
Monkey Grip   COC 59102
(Bill Wyman solo album)
I Wanna Get Me A Gun
Crazy Woman
Pussy
Mighty Fine Time
Monkey Grip Glue
What A Blow
White Lightnin'
I'll Pull You Thro'
It's A Wonder

October 1974
It's Only Rock 'n' Roll   COC 79101
If You Can't Rock Me
Ain't Too Proud To Beg
It's Only Rock 'n' Roll
Till The Next Goodbye
Time Waits For No One
Luxury
Dance Little Sister
If You Really Want To Be My Friend
Short And Curlies
Fingerprint File

June 1975
Metamorphosis   ABKCO ANA 1
Out Of Time
Don't Lie To Me
Each And Every Day Of The Year
Heart Of Stone
I'd Much Rather Be With The Boys
Try A Little Harder
I Don't Know Why
If You Let Me
Jiving Sister Fanny
Downtown Suzie
Family
Memo From Turner
I'm Going Down

June 1975
Made In The Shade   COC 79101
Brown Sugar
Tumbling Dice
Happy
Dance Little Sister
Wild Horses
Angie
Bitch
It's Only Rock 'n' Roll
Doo Doo Doo Doo Doo (Heartbreaker)
Rip This Joint

February 1976
Stone Alone   COC 79103
(Bill Wyman solo)
A Quarter To Three
Gimme Just One Chance
Soul Satisfying
Apache Woman
Every Sixty Seconds
Get It On
Feet
Peanut Butter Time
Wine And Wimmen
If You Wanna Be Happy
What's The Point
No More Foolin'

April 1976
Black & Blue   COC 79104
Hot Stuff
Hand Of Fate
Cherry Oh Baby
Memory Motel
Hey Negrita
Melody
Fool To Cry
Crazy Mama

September 1977
Love You Live   COC 2-90701
Intro
Honky Tonk Women
If You Can't Rock Me
Get Off Of My Cloud
Happy
Hot Stuff
Star, Star
Tumbling Dice
Fingerprint File
You Gotta Move
You Can't Always Get What You Want
Mannish Boy
Crackin' Up
Little Red Rooster
Around And Around
It's Only Rock 'n' Roll
Brown Sugar
Jumpin' Jack Flash
Sympathy For The Devil

June 1978
Some Girls   CUN 39108
Miss You
When The Whip Comes Down
Imagination
Some Girls
Lies
Far Away Eyes
Respectable
Before They Make Me Run
Beast Of Burden
Shattered

June 1980
Emotional Rescue   CUN 39111
Dance
Summer Romance
Send It To Me
Let Me Go
Indian Girl
Where The Boys Go
Down The Hole
Emotional Rescue
She's So Cold
All About You

September 1981
Tattoo You   CUN 39114
Start Me Up
Hang Fire
Slave
Little T & A
Black Limousine
Neighbours
Worried About You
Tops
Heaven
No Use In Crying
Waiting On A Friend

June 1982
Still Life   CUN 39115
Under My Thumb
Let's Spend The Night Together
Shattered
Twenty Flight Rock
Going To A Go Go
Let Me Go
Time Is On My Side
Imagination
Start Me Up
Satisfaction

Filmography

1964   **Teenage Command Performance**
(The TAMI Show)
Director: Steve Binder

1965   **Charlie Is My Darling**
Two days on tour in Ireland
Director: Peter Whitehead

1966   **Mord und Totschar (A Degree of Murder)**
Starring Anita Pallenberg; music by Brian Jones
Director: Volker Schlondorff

1967   **Tonite Let's All Make Love In London**
A 'Swinging London' investigation
Director: Peter Whitehead

1968   **One Plus One/Sympathy For The Devil**
Director: Jean-Luc Godard

1969   **Michael Kohlhaas – Der Rebell**
Starring Anita Pallenberg and Keith Richard
Director: Volker Schlondorff

1969   **Invocation Of My Demon Brother**
Music by Mick Jagger
Director: Kenneth Anger

1970   **Ned Kelly**
Starring Mick Jagger
Director: Tony Richardson

1970   **Performance**
Starring James Fox and Mick Jagger
Directors: Nic Roeg and Donald Cammell

1970   **Gimme Shelter**
1969 Tour and Altamont
Directors: David and Albert Maysles and Charlotte Zwerin

1974   **Ladies and Gentlemen The Rolling Stones**
A record of the concert at Fort Worth, Texas, 24 June 1972
Director: Rollin Binzar

Bibliography

Roy Carr: *The Rolling Stones: An Illustrated Record* New
  English Library, London, 1976
David Dalton ed.: *The Rolling Stones: An Unauthorised
  Biography* Quick Fox, New York, 1979
David Dalton ed.: *The Rolling Stones: The First Twenty
  Years* Thames and Hudson, London, 1982
Peter Goddard: *The Rolling Stones Live* Sidgwick and
Jackson, London, 1982
Pete F. Goodman: *Our Own Story by The Rolling Stones*
  Corgi, London, 1964
Robert Greenfield: *A Journey Through America with The
  Rolling Stones* Panther, London, 1975
Tony Jasper: *The Rolling Stones* Octopus, London, 1975
Phillip C. Luce: *The Stones* Allen Wingate-Baker, London,
  1970
J. Marks: *Mick Jagger* Abacus, London, 1974
Miles: *The Rolling Stones File* Music Sales Ltd, London,
  1976
Miles: *The Rolling Stones: An Illustrated Discography*
  Omnibus, London, 1980
Miles: *Mick Jagger In His Own Words* Omnibus, London,
  1982
Jeremy Pascall: *The Rolling Stones,* Hamlyn, London, 1977
The Rolling Stone Interviews Arthur Barker, London, 1980
Tony Sanchez: *Up And Down With The Rolling Stones*
  Morrow, New York, 1979

Anthony Scaduto: *Mick Jagger* W. H. Allen, London, 1974
George Tremlett: *The Rolling Stones Story* Futura, London, 1974